Mother tongue to English

The young child in the multicultural school

DAPHNE M. BROWN

CAMBRIDGE UNIVERSITY PRESS
CAMBRIDGE
LONDON · NEW YORK · MELBOURNE

Published by the Syndics of the Cambridge University Press
The Pitt Building, Trumpington Street, Cambridge CB2 1RP
Bentley House, 200 Euston Road, London NW1 2DB
32 East 57th Street, New York, NY 10022, USA
296 Beaconsfield Parade, Middle Park, Melbourne 3206, Australia

© Cambridge University Press 1979

First published 1979

Printed in Great Britain
at the University Press, Cambridge

Library of Congress Cataloguing in Publication Data
Brown, Daphne M, 1934–
Mother tongue to English.
Bibliography: p.
Includes index.
1. Education, Bilingual. 2. Children — Language.
3. Native language and education. I. Title.
LC 3715.B76   371.9'7   77-83987
ISBN 0 521 21873 X hard covers
ISBN 0 521 29299 9 paperback

Dedicated to Win

my invaluable friend and colleague
whose unfailing support for twenty-one years
has made my work and this book possible

'I have forgotten the word
I intended to say, and
my thought, unembodied
returns to the realm
of shadows'

(O. Mandelstam)

They do not understand
the words I speak, and
my thought, unembodied
returns to the realm
of shadows

I do not know the
words to say, and
my thought, unembodied
returns to the realm
of shadows

Contents

Acknowledgements

My sincere appreciation must be expressed to the many colleagues, students and friends who through their keen interest in my work and lectures have persuaded me to transfer my thoughts, observations and experience from the spoken to the printed word.

I am especially grateful to Margaret L. Peters MA PhD for her wise counsel and constant encouragement throughout my year at the Cambridge Institute of Education and during the writing of this book.

My thanks are also due to the Hertfordshire Education Authority for granting me a year's secondment which gave me the opportunity to carry out detailed case-studies of two young children learning English as a second language. I am indebted to the headmistress and the staff of the infant school which these children attended, and in particular the two class teachers who enabled me to observe Suba and Asad without interruption and whose unfailing help and co-operation made the case-studies possible.

My gratitude must also be expressed to Edie Garvie and Evelyn Davies BA for their constructive recommendations concerning the manuscripts and the advice and support which they have so readily given to me.

This book could not have been written in its present form without the untiring work and patience of all my staff at Hillshott, in particular Madhu Joshi whose gift of deep friendship and ability to speak several languages have been the source of true communication between people of different cultures in and around our school. The ideas and practical experience of Pauline Lean and Raymonde Kipling with children in our language group play a major part in this book, and Phyllis Croyle and Gladys Walker have given much time and effort in the typing of the manuscripts — my sincere gratitude to all of them.

Finally I must thank the children of many different cultures and creeds who during the past twenty-one years have brought joy and purpose into my life and taught me to care, as together we have shared both the privileges and the problems of learning to live and speak in a multicultural society.   D.M.B.

Introduction

The first day of the September term had begun and forty six-year-old children straggled into the classroom. They were all strangers to me and, as a newcomer to the school, I was anxious for us to introduce ourselves as quickly as possible for I had much to discover and a great deal to learn.

The children found no difficulty in telling me who they were and where they lived and, in spite of the fact that their responses to my questions were often phrased in ungrammatical jargon, I was able immediately to understand what they were trying to say, and form an initial relationship with them.

Suddenly, the flow of conversation abruptly halted. Two boys in the front row showed little, if any, interest in what was being said; their sallow skins and dark hair singled them out from the other children, and so did the vacant expressions on their faces as they watched me silently. 'What is your name?' I asked. 'Petros Petrou.' 'And yours?' 'Nicholas Nicolau.' 'And have you any brothers or sisters?' — a voice from behind sharply intervened. 'Miss — 'e can't talk no English — 'e don't know what yer sayin', 'e don't understand.'

This incident took place over twenty years ago, but the impact of that introductory meeting with those two Greek boys left an impression which still to this day remains vividly in my memory.

During the nineteen-fifties, teachers applying for positions in the Inner London Borough of Islington were aware of the poor housing conditions from which many of the children came — it was a known fact that some of the worst living accommodation in London was to be found in this area. Before accepting my new appointment, I had been warned about the severity of the psychological and physical problems which children from these deprived backgrounds were encountering, but no one had given me the slightest indication that I might be faced with the challenge of teaching a child who was unable to speak English; a child to whom even a simple phrase appeared to be incomprehensible in spite of carefully chosen words and deliberate clarity of speech.

I was a young teacher with only three years' experience and my first thought at that time was for myself. How could I occupy these boys? How could I possibly teach them anything, where should I begin? And — the thought which was uppermost in my mind — how could I discipline them and try to control the other children at the same time? As far as I can remember, hardly any consideration was given to the children's feelings — there was no time to try to understand what they were endeavouring to communicate to me in their own language, and both boys were thrust into the classroom activities with little thought as to whether they understood what was happening around them. If they were occupied and appeared to be happy they were left alone while I concentrated on the children who could easily tell me what they wanted and who responded quickly to my suggestions and requests. I was frustrated by my futile efforts to communicate with Petros and Nicholas — verbal explanations proved ineffectual even on the few occasions when their nodding heads indicated an element of understanding, and the joy of story-telling was marred by the constant appeals, from the children and me, asking the boys to sit still, be quiet and listen!

For weeks the two boys sat drawing pictures or copying words because I had neither the experience, the knowledge, the insight nor the time needed to impart the necessary basic skills which would enable them to extend their faculties into the realms of mathematics or verbal and written expression work. Placed in the care of a well-meaning but ill-equipped teacher, they were left to their own devices in the hope that eventually they would 'pick up' the English language from the indigenous children by grasping the local restricted vocabulary and phraseology whenever it could be linked with their experience and understanding.

Petros and Nicholas proved to be the first of many hundreds of children who have passed through my hands and for whom English is a second language. The children's nationalities, mother tongues, cultures, creeds and customs have been of a wide variety, and the multicultural schools where we have met and worked together have each had different methods, organisations and forms of relationships according to the needs and personalities of the people in the communities they served.

Although some excellent in-service courses are now provided on 'the education of minority groups' and 'teaching English as a second language', there are still areas throughout the country where little help is available. I had to interview college students for a teaching post in

my school. It was not an easy task to short list the applicants, having
a very large number from which to choose. I finally selected eight, one
of my criteria being that, because of the college or place where they
trained, I imagined that they would have had some knowledge or experience of E2L* children. Out of the eight, five had had responsibility for
children with limited English during a teaching practice, but only two
had had any information on E2L children during their three-year
course, and one of these had only been given a single lecture on the subject covering all nationalities and age ranges!

Infant and nursery teachers are still frequently caught unawares
when a young child speaking very limited English is suddenly placed
in their care. I meet and discuss the problems with many who are experiencing the same sense of inadequacy as I did a generation ago, and
this is not surprising because so little consideration has been given to
the difficulties arising with E2L children in this particular age group.

Many reports on education in the past have ignored the needs of
children speaking very limited English in the infant school, and when
reference has been made to them, it has implied that the children 'pick
up' the second language without any problem, and the teachers have
little or no difficulty in dealing with this added responsibility.

In the Plowden Report, we read in the paragraph referring to immigrant children:

It is absolutely essential to overcome the language barrier. This is less serious for
a child entering the infant school. He rapidly acquires, both in the classroom and
outside, a good command of the relatively limited number of words, phrases and
sentences in common use among the other children. He can then learn to read with
the rest by normal methods.
(Central Advisory Council for Education 1967, p.71.)

Does the child in the infant school rapidly acquire a *good* command of
English as a second language if left to 'pick it up' from the other children? What emotional, psychological, physical and mental pressures
are put upon him whilst trying to achieve this tremendous expectation?
What effect does the traumatic experience of entering school for the
first time have upon both the present and future life of the child? He
not only has to undergo the initial separation from his family but, in
addition, has to face an entirely different cultural environment. He

* See terminology p.5.

cannot understand what is being said, and is unable to make himself understood. Few, if any, respond to his previously intelligible speech.

Fortunately the more recent Bullock report has an enlightened and positive view of the needs of the child having to learn English as a second language in the infant and nursery school. Special reference is made to this age group. Provision of nursery classes is seen as having great importance for the early language development and social needs of children of overseas parentage. The report then adds:

Teachers of these young children have shown reluctance to do any 'formal' language work with them, usually on the ground that in the good infant or nursery class they would learn to speak English anyway, without any intervention on the teacher's part . . . To meet the special needs of these children, teachers in nursery and infant classes should be willing to modify their traditional organisation.
(Department of Education and Science 1976, p.292.)

How and why should the traditional organisation be modified?

The content and conclusions in this book are based entirely on my own first-hand experience in multicultural infant schools, and substantiated by a case-study of two Indian boys which I was able to undertake during a period of secondment at the Cambridge Institute of Education.

The main aim of the book is to develop in the reader a sensitive awareness towards the needs of young children from ethnic minority groups, particularly those who are having to learn English as a second language, and to provide a positive approach towards helping them during their early years in school. Special attention is given to the difficulties which arise where the number of children of overseas parentage is comparatively small. Situations in this category are increasing because many families are moving away from the larger parent communities which are often found in the inner cities.

The book is divided into three parts:

(1) The young child in the multicultural school, based on my experience in five multicultural schools during twenty-one years as a class and head teacher.
(2) Closer observation: the findings of a detailed case-study concerning Suba and Asad, two young brothers unable to speak English and placed in normal infant school classes.
(3) Practical recommendations: suggestions for teachers based on the work in my present school.

Terminology

For the purpose of clarifying many of the issues raised, it is essential to differentiate between the various cultural and language categories to which the children belong. In order to do this the terminology I have used should be defined in this book as follows:

Immigrant child — a child living in England but whose birthplace, culture and mother tongue are foreign; one who has to learn and/or fully develop English as a second language after his admission to school.

E2L child — a child who was born in England but whose mother tongue is not English; one who has to learn and/or fully develop English as a second language after his admission to school.

Bilingual child — a child who speaks English and another language fluently and well.

Indigenous child — a child who is born in England and whose mother tongue is English.

PART ONE

The young child in the multicultural school

1 The new admission

Kulwinder whimpered as she stood rigidly by the classroom door clutching my hand. She had never seen the inside of the school before and it was very probable that this was the first occasion on which she had been taken from her mother by an English person. Knowing a little about her home and culture I could safely assume that she had never handled paint, clay or manipulative toys, and her experience of group play with English children using water or a home corner similar to the one in the classroom, would be virtually non-existent. Neither of Kulwinder's parents spoke English, therefore the language flowing around her was unintelligible — a confused babble of sounds. The reassuring, comforting words of the teacher were meaningless to this child who had been suddenly uprooted from her familiar surroundings with little preparation, for her parents too were bewildered by the unfamiliar equipment and bustle of an English infant school.

Kulwinder was not forced into the classroom. She was quietly taken to another room where a few pieces of basic equipment were attractively arranged. There she met children who spoke her language and the jumbled sounds suddenly became meaningful as she watched them play and experiment together. The whimpering gradually stopped although it re-occurred daily for a month, and continued incessantly when she had to return to the 'normal' classroom during the afternoon.

I remember an Indian child who tearfully 'droned' for nearly a year in a school where there was no withdrawal group. Other children of different nationalities placed in similar circumstances have remained silent for as long as two years. Adult comments concerning these withdrawn reactions have referred to ' "culture shock" which will be cured in time when the child has adapted to his new surroundings' or 'the fact that the child is listening and taking in — hopefully one day he will give out'.

The listening, pre-speaking period is an essential attribute in the acquisition of a new language (Derrick 1966), but the teacher must be aware of the subtle differences between the silent child who is actively

listening to and absorbing the new sound patterns he hears whilst feeling secure and happy in his new surroundings, and the child who remains withdrawn and insecure due to his inability to cope with the rich
environment and the expectations of those around him.

Considerable time, energy, money and research have been given to
establishing ways in which children can be transferred from the home
to the school with comparative ease. The need for the child to feel secure is the hub on which the varied activities and attitudes of all concerned revolve. Links between the home and school are encouraged and
fostered in order to help the child to adjust as quickly and with as little
difficulty as possible.

The difference between the school and the home background of a
minority-group child is often much greater than that encountered by
an English child. Although these differences are obvious and very familiar to teachers experienced in this field, it is important that we should
remind ourselves from time to time of the additional adaptations which
some immigrant and E2L children have to make.

Material differences

Play equipment

The indigenous children are more likely to be familiar with the utensils,
clothing, cutlery, 'food' and equipment in the home corner (depend-
ing, of course, on the culture and customs of the immigrant or E2L
child, and the provision made by the class teacher — see p.106). Bricks,
Lego and constructional toys are new to some immigrant or E2L children; they may never have known the satisfaction of building and bal-
ancing with these particular materials, creating width and height, and
then destroying them with a masterful blow. Paint and clay are often
unknown mediums and sometimes found to be repugnant; they may
be left untouched for a long time. Jigsaw puzzles remain a mystery until time reveals their hidden secrets through sight and touch (see p.86).

Books

The books provided in an English infant school contain illustrations
which are designed and presented in ways which may be unfamiliar to
a child of Eastern origin and background, and the print consists of
strange signs bearing little resemblance to the symbols used in letters,

papers and other reading matter in his own home. I have found that some young immigrant and E2L children have considerable difficulty in re-orientating their perceptual-motor skills to the classroom materials. Could this be because, although the children may not be able to read themselves, their observations of their parents' writing, the way in which they read, and the books, magazines and papers they use and enjoy, are so different from those found in school? (See pp.86—7.)

Some immigrant and E2L children do not know how to handle books simply because they have never before had the opportunity to do so — particularly if their mothers are illiterate.

The language barrier

Not only will a non-English speaking child be unable to comprehend the teacher, but he may not be able to make himself understood even when he needs to go to the toilet. He cannot communicate with other children, unless there are others who speak his language; he cannot ask any questions; he cannot express or explain his feelings to anyone. He cannot, through language, share in any discussions, stories or rhymes, however carefully they are linked with his home experiences. Although he has the ability to talk, any effort to do so fails miserably and, perhaps for the first time in his life, he is unable to invoke a satisfactory response to his speech. A five-year-old may not be able to comprehend the concept of a 'language' or appreciate that the sounds being made by those around him are a method of communication (see p.62). He has to realise that people fail to respond to his utterances because they cannot understand what he is saying and not because they do not like or love him.

The sense of helplessness felt when nursing a weeping child who cannot speak English is only understood by those who have been placed in such a situation when no word of comfort or reassurance can be given and the cause of the distress is unknown. A child sobbing for his mother, or crying because he is in pain, is a pathetic little figure when he cannot explain how he feels or receive any consolation. Misunderstanding such as this can lead to practical difficulties such as soiled underclothes or unexpected vomiting. Children who have fallen or been hurt may find it difficult in their state of shock to indicate the injured place when they simply cannot tell you where it is or what happened. It is easy in such circumstances to wash a grubby knee and leave a hidden bump or badly grazed hip unattended.

Older children are usually capable of finding alternative methods in order to make themselves understood in an emergency, but young children in the infant school, particularly those new to the surroundings, usually resort to tears beyond which it is sometimes impossible to penetrate.

A new cultural environment

Many five-year-old immigrant and E2L children will adapt comparatively easily to the school routine and eagerly experiment with the wealth of new equipment in a responsible manner. Others will rush from one exciting area to another, not knowing how to control their play and unable to settle anywhere for any length of time. Those who are used to being formally directed by their parents, stand, waiting to be told what to do and where to go, afraid to do the wrong thing and afraid to get dirty. The indigenous children often react in similar ways but they can be encouraged and guided by the teacher's appropriate remarks, unlike the non-English speaking child who, frightened and bewildered, may stand on the fringe of the activities with little to reassure him and forge a familiar link with home and family, in spite of all that research and reason recommend.

Some immigrant and E2L children may have to adapt to a very different relationship with their teacher from the one they have formed with adults in their own community (Cheetham 1972). Parental expectations and methods of discipline vary enormously. Corporal punishment, times of stillness and silence, types and the purpose of play, and forms of expression through voice, music, movement, laughter or tears can be completely different from the expectations of the teacher and the organisation within the classroom. There are greater differences in dress, jewelry, manners, food, seating, religion, forms of worship, cosmetics, odours and hair styles between the parents of minority-group children and their teacher, than between the wide cross-section of English parents and the adults in the school.

Discipline

The immigrant parents sometimes have very formal ideas about education, particularly on the opportunities allowed for play. They may not have attended school themselves and their children are totally unprepared for the lively, free-moving atmosphere of a modern infant reception class.

West Indian grandmothers have said to me on several occasions: 'I have taught him at least one thing, and that is to be quiet.' An experienced, well-qualified teacher from Jamaica explained to me that it was often the 'caring' parents who strongly believed in corporal punishment for their children. His own mother used this method of discipline with the firm conviction that 'The more you beat the bottom, the better the brain.'

A young West Indian boy arrived in my class one day direct from Jamaica. Although he often spoke to me I could not understand anything he said and he, in turn, appeared to be unable to respond to any of my requests however encouraging or firm my tone of voice sounded. After six weeks I contacted his grandmother and explained my difficulties to her as gently as I could. 'Do not worry,' she reassured me. 'I am so sorry. I will beat him and beat him until he reads.' I pleaded with her to refrain from taking such action, but in vain. On the following morning Stephen approached me. 'I read,' he announced with a clarity I had thought impossible, and read he did! From that day onwards Stephen was hardly ever seen without a book, and he quickly learnt to read fluently. (In this particular instance a different form of discipline appeared to solve certain difficulties in communication, but dialect interference could have been the cause of the problem, in which case administering corporal punishment could have proved disastrous.)

In my own experience I have found that the present generation of children are beaten much less frequently than their parents were in their childhood, but cases do continue to arise from time to time, sometimes quite unexpectedly. Recently I discovered that a six-year-old child in my school was being given an hour's homework every evening by her parents. If she failed to complete the exercise to their satisfaction she was beaten because, her father explained, 'this is how I learnt and I want the best education for my daughter'.

Dress

Clothing in a multicultural school can add colour and interest to the drabbest of classrooms if the individual nationalities are allowed to wear the design and material of their own choice and race. Providing the style is not dangerous, inhibiting or unsuitable for our climate, I allow the children in my school to dress as naturally as possible. Not only do their individual selections of colour enhance the children's inherited features, but the various styles seem to blend with their physique and movements, particularly those of the young girls. Some immigrant children who have to adapt suddenly to wearing a school uniform may feel hampered at first and restricted in their movements, although, of course, they quickly adjust to their new attire.

Clothes are a natural talking point between both children and adults. When an immigrant or E2L child is admitted to school we may not be able to converse with either him or members of his family, but it is always possible to admire their dress and when such a gesture is made towards the mothers or grandmothers the contact is usually rewarded with a smile. Many illiterate mothers are excellent at sewing, embroidery or knitting, they have good reason to be proud of their handiwork and warmly appreciate approval.

Footwear is sometimes an added problem to the families from hot climates where children are accustomed to going barefoot. The Indian children with whom I work nearly always have bare feet from choice when I visit them in their homes.

The weather affects everyone, but I felt an added sympathy for the West Indian who expressed her disappointment to me one bright winter's morning. 'Oh,' she said, 'the sun is shining at last, but it is a cold sun. We never have a cold sun at home, it is always hot.'

Birthdays

The correct dates of birth frequently pose problems in the multicultural infant school and birth certificates are helpful. Even so, the teachers should appreciate what circumstances may lie behind the lack of a birth certificate if the child has come from abroad, and how easily misunderstandings can arise.

Some nationalities count their babies as one year old at birth. I have frequently had to remedy this calculation in the past with Greek, Turkish and Italian families. Many Asian children do not have birth certificates or surnames (as used in the English culture) until they apply for their passports and I believe that because of this, some birth certificates may be inaccurate. If a baby is born in a mountainous area during the rainy season, a registrar is not going to journey for miles to record his birth, and nor are his parents — a few weeks or even months here or there make no difference in these circumstances. I asked a father once the date of birth of his newly admitted boy and the answer I received was 'I cannot tell, he was born at harvest time when the moon was high' — there are indeed problems and difficulties on both sides!

It is important for the teacher to know which celebrations are recognised in the culture with which she is involved. Indian children are not always accustomed to celebrating their birthdays, they may not know the dates and it is very possible that they will not receive any cards or presents, although this practice is now being introduced in order to conform with the English custom. In contrast to this, a little touch which I have appreciated in the Italian community is when, on the occasion of a baby's baptism, I have received a tiny basket of sugared almonds. Foreknowledge of customs and festivals can help a teacher to gain a deeper insight into the way of life of the new children in her care, and give her greater understanding of their reactions.

All these comparatively small differences can mount up in the mind of a newly admitted immigrant or E2L child, and instead of enjoying his first days at school he can become withdrawn and silent. I have known minority-group children go through an infant school without speaking, and no special help has been given to them. Whilst attending a conference on 'teaching English as a second language', the head of the English department in a comprehensive school told us how desperate she had become over two Asian girls who, after eighteen months' tuition, still refused to speak a word of English. The teacher's reaction was a natural one, but so often we fail to appreciate the cause for such a negative response from children. Some help and understanding is now given to such pupils in the senior school, but, what provision is being made for children in the infant and nursery classes? Should they really be expected to learn a new language without specialised help, and cope with strange cultural adaptations without any specific guidance? What can the teacher in the infant school do to ensure that the minority-group children in her class, and in particular those who cannot speak English, adjust to their new way of life as easily and as well as possible without undue stress and strain?

2 One day, one child – Ravinder

'In this open-plan school the children of all ages mix freely. We have found that this freedom with its natural interaction and communication helps the few children with language difficulties to develop their English surprisingly quickly.' – a headteacher.
(Brittan and Townsend 1972, p.24.)

One afternoon I met with a headmistress of a multicultural infant school to discuss and share mutual problems, and the methods and organisation which we used to try and alleviate them within our schools.

It was not long before I learned in no uncertain terms that the policy within her school was to accept the immigrant and E2L children without any special consideration and leave them to 'absorb the English language naturally while working among the other children in the normal class situation. These "immigrant" children are no trouble in our school,' she assured me; 'In fact they are often easier to manage than the English children – I certainly would never consider segregating them into a language group, even for part of the day – that would only cause trouble with both sets of parents. No, leave them alone, and they soon learn to adjust.'

I asked if I might visit the school and did so on a number of occasions. I watched several children who could not speak English wandering quietly around and the headmistress willingly allowed me to record the movements of one such child throughout a day. Ravinder was an attractive Asian boy, six years of age, who had attended school for four weeks.

9.00 a.m.
Ravinder entered the school with his brother and then walked alone to the cloakroom and hence to his classroom. He stood in a corner and paused, watching the other children greeting their friends and wending their way to the carpeted area where they sat or knelt together.

Ravinder walked silently over to the carpet and sat down. Almost immediately he knelt up, watching the children talking amongst themselves. He leaned over and looked at a child who was studying an illustrated story book, then kneeling back on to his heels he finally relaxed into a sitting position waiting for the teacher to call the register. He watched her face intently. 'Ravinder.' 'Yes' — his expression remained unchanged as he replied to his name.

9.12 a.m.

The teacher discussed the organisation of the groups for the day and commented on particular pieces of work which needed to be completed. Ravinder's group began the morning with an activity period of the children's individual choice, and paint, Lego, water, bricks, sand and the home corner were made available. The children clambered to their feet and dispersed throughout the room and into the corridor, each one intent on equipping himself for a specific task and finding a suitable place in which to carry it out.

Ravinder stood up, walked past the window and tossed the venetian blind cord. Ignoring the paint and sand, the home corner and the bricks, he wandered over to his drawer, pulled it open and took out his writing book.

He walked over to the tin of pencils, selected one and then, after inspecting it carefully, dropped it back into the tin. He picked up a carton of wax crayons and carried it with his writing book over to a table at one end of the room. He sat down facing the wall with his back to the class.

9.20 a.m.

Ravinder turned to a page on which the teacher had previously written some figures and counted to himself 'one, two, three, four, five, six'. He wrote '6' and then twisted and turned the crayon between his fingers, moving it up and down. He turned to a different page and again studied the figures 1 to 6, this time written in his own handwriting, and counted 'one, two, three, four, five, six'. On yet another page he counted four gummed shapes which had been stuck adjacent a large '5'; it was unfortunate that only the grubby outline of the fifth shape remained. 'One, two, three, four . . . one'; he paused to look at the next figure — a '2' accompanied by one gummed shape.

9.22 a.m.

Ravinder crayoned a stroke on the table and rubbed it away with his finger. He looked at the words on the wall — they were the names of different colours — and then turned and watched the teacher working in the corner of the room where a group of children were writing.

He stood up and walked over to the pencil tin, this time he selected the one on which his name was written, and returned to the table holding it between his fingers. He opened his book and turned over several pages, finally stopping at one which already contained some writing. He copied the figures 5 to 10 from the wall cards, and then, turning over wrote 1 to 10 glancing quickly at the cards between each number.

9.26 a.m.

Ravinder sat looking into space.

9.28 a.m.
He copied the figures 1 to 10.

9.30 a.m.
He sat looking at the table.

9.31 a.m.
He turned to another page and wrote the figures 1 to 10, this time without copying.

9.35 a.m.
He sat looking into space.

9.37 a.m.
He wrote 1 to 5 silently.

9.38 a.m.
He sat looking into space.

9.39 a.m.
He turned and watched the group of children with the teacher.

9.40 a.m.
He wrote 7 to 10, silently.

9.41 a.m.
An English boy opened the classroom door, Ravinder glanced round and looked at him and then returned to his book. He wrote 1 to 10, silently.

9.42 a.m.
He counted aloud 1 to 10.

9.45 a.m.
He wrote 1 to 10, and counted aloud.

9.47 a.m.
He sat and watched the teacher, and sucking his pencil he shook his head from side to side.

9.53 a.m.
He dropped his pencil, picked it up and watched the teacher again.

9.55 a.m.
He sat with his head on his arms leaning on the back of his chair.

9.57 a.m.
He drew a line in his book.

9.58 a.m.
He stood up and walked over to two English boys who were playing dominoes.
The boys were concentrating hard on their game and ignored Ravinder who
watched them intently. He appeared to notice every move they made, and
the varying expressions on their faces — as one boy smiled, Ravinder smiled. He
listened to their conversation — 'A one or a five.' 'Oh, a seven or a one.' 'We've
got to go round the corner.' 'Two fives or a blank.' 'Can't.' Ravinder flicked his
lips with his thumb. 'Your turn.' 'Whoops, that's six.' 'Look.' 'Can't go . . . Let's
have another game.'

10.05 a.m.
The boys packed the dominoes into a box and placed it on a shelf.Ravinder stood
and watched — they did not appear to be aware of his presence as they walked
away leaving him standing alone by an empty table.

Ravinder stared at the group of children around the teacher and then returning
to his book he sat down once again. He folded back the corner of a page and wrote
1 to 5, after which he closed the book, and reaching out to an eraser which hung,
suspended from the wall by a piece of string, he vigorously rubbed a few marks
from the cover. An English child sat down next to him — he also used the eraser
and then proceeded to write but, although he was almost touching Ravinder, there
was no attempt to communicate in any way.

10.10 a.m.
Ravinder stood up, put away his pencil and book and went to the toilet.

10.13 a.m.
Ravinder emerged from the toilet and, pausing in the doorway, he watched two
boys playing with bricks in the corridor. One turned and spoke to him. 'You're
not coming out here. You go back into the classroom, you'll muck up our building.' (These were the first words which any child had spoken to Ravinder that
morning.) He stood and watched, and smiled.

10.15 a.m.
Ravinder returned to the classroom, he walked over to the shop and, pressing the
keys of the till, he watched the numbers flicking up. The teacher told the children
to pack up. Ravinder continued to experiment with the keys until suddenly he
heard the bell ring.

10.25 a.m.
He dropped the till and ran to the cloakroom, catching hold of an English girl's
hand (a retarded eight-year-old). 'Come on!' he cried and pulled her along the
corridor. He stood on a bench and peering over the partition watched her
putting on her coat — a smile spread across his face.

An English boy entered the cloakroom, Ravinder turned and smiled at him, but
was completely ignored as the boy rushed past, twisted round and raced outside.
Ravinder stretched out his arms to the boy, but there was no response.

The eight-year-old girl walked down the corridor. Ravinder chased her into a corner behind a door. He pushed her, his hands on her shoulders and then pulled her towards him. He pinched her face and stamped on her toe. He swung the door back and shut her in the corner — leaving her, he ran back to the cloakroom.

The girl walked solemnly towards the playground. An English and a West Indian boy entered the cloakroom, pulled their coats off the pegs and raced down the corridor. Ravinder ran after them but was left behind. Another English boy, Martin (a less able child), sauntered down the corridor alongside Ravinder. Ravinder took his hand and together they walked into the playground.

In the playground
Ravinder chased Martin round the climbing frame, but Martin ran away.

Ravinder stood still, saw an English boy from his class and ran towards him, but the boy ran away.

He leaned against a tree trunk alone.

Martin ran up to him, hit him, and ran away again. Ravinder watched Martin playing with the other children — they all ran round the tree trunk, but there was no communication with Ravinder as he leaned against it.

Four children played round him, hiding and 'shooting' as they passed him by. Ravinder held out his hands to Martin, who shrugged his shoulders and ran away. Ravinder strolled across the playground with his hands in his pockets.

The bell rang. He ran to his class line, held hands with Martin and smiled, they walked to the cloakroom.

As Ravinder went to his peg he appeared deliberately to knock three children with his elbow; he then wandered into the classroom and went straight to the cupboard and removed the box of milk straws. Ravinder held out the straws to a West Indian boy who pushed them away. Martin walked over to him and together they placed the straws into the milk bottles, and then distributed the milk. Five children said 'Thank you', otherwise there was no comment.

10.55 a.m.
Ravinder drank his milk and after returning the empty bottle he wandered aimlessly around the room for a few minutes, and then went to the box of plastic Meccano. He carefully fastened some pieces together and made a truck — he smiled as he examined the finished article. A West Indian boy came up to him and pulled the model out of his hands. Ravinder pulled it back. 'Tch,' remarked the West Indian boy and briskly walked away.

11.07 a.m.
Ravinder continued to play with the Meccano, and Martin joined him. Ravinder was searching in a box of pieces for a particular nut and whilst he was thus engaged Martin played with the truck. Ravinder pulled the model away and placed it carefully in the box where it could be under his watchful eye while he continued his search, with one hand remaining firmly on the vehicle. The required nut was located, and Martin then helped Ravinder lift the model out of the box.

Ravinder made a rod and tapped Martin gently, Martin ignored him and Ravinder continued working with a collection of tiny pieces — his lips moved, but there was no sound.

11.20 a.m.
The class teacher called to Ravinder. 'Ravinder, will you bring your reading book
to me.' Ravinder fetched a Ladybird Picture Book 1 and repeated the words after
the teacher as they looked at the illustrations. 'Train, paper, tree, . . . '

They were interrupted by another child. Ravinder waited. 'Ducks, ship-boat,
gloves, flowers, orange,' Ravinder smiled, 'lollipop.' 'You eat it,' the teacher
explained. 'Keys, egg, telephone, cow, . . . ' The words continued, but after five
minutes six children had gathered round waiting for the teacher's help, interrupt-
ing her with their requests.

The teacher left Ravinder in order to supervise them. He sat, turning the pages
of the book quickly and on reaching the back cover he fetched a second book
from his drawer.

The teacher returned and together they repeated the names of twenty-one
objects; five other children stood round to listen. Ravinder returned to the first
book, and began to name some of the illustrations; three more children joined
the group of five.

(It appeared that as soon as the teacher focused her attention upon Ravinder,
certain children immediately clamoured for help. This happened frequently during
my observations of Suba when he, not other children, was being given special assistance by the teacher.)

The teacher and Ravinder named twelve more objects and then the teacher
pointed to Ravinder's writing book, and indicated that she wanted him to copy
some of the pictures and words. Ravinder began to write. One of the original
domino players watched him. 'Look, he hasn't drawn the picture, he's only writing
the words,' he commented, pointing to Ravinder's book and touching the teacher.
The boy then turned over one of the pages and deliberately (but not unkindly)
placed the crayon tin over the illustration of a ball; 'Can you read that?' he implied
without speaking. Ravinder wrote 'ball' and the boy walked away.

Ravinder rubbed the blue and orange crayons together.

The teacher turned over another page and Ravinder wrote 'ball'. He drew a tiny
ball beside the writing and then sat still. He was apparently waiting for the teacher
to turn over another page!

11.50 a.m.
'Draw a picture, Ravinder, draw me a picture,' the teacher suggested. Ravinder
picked up his pencil and wrote 'cot'. The teacher was holding some flash cards;
she called over to Ravinder, 'Ravinder, can you read these?' Ravinder looked up.
'Peter, Jane, tree, and,' he answered without any hesitation and without any
illustrations to help him.

12 noon
The children packed up their activities and left the classroom; on seeing everyone
disappear through the door, Ravinder gathered up his books, placed them in his
drawer and went to dinner.

1.15 p.m.

The children entered the classroom and sat on the carpet. Ravinder walked in alone.
A child had brought a model of a horse to school and the children were feeling its
tail which was made from real hair. Ravinder stroked it. A West Indian boy pushed
the horse away, but the teacher intervened, 'Let Ravinder feel its tail.' The horse
was passed to Ravinder, but immediately removed from his hands by an Indian
child.

The teacher told the children which group activities were going to take place.
'Ravinder, would you like to play snakes and ladders?' Ravinder made no response.
'Who will show Ravinder how to play? Maureen? No — all right — John?'

1.30 p.m.

John caught hold of Ravinder's hand and led him to a table arranged with a board,
dice and counters. 'I'm going to play too,' shouted Michael, a West Indian boy,
clambering over to join in the game.

John and Ravinder sat down next to one another and Michael stood beside
them. Michael shook the dice three times and then John had his turn. 'Now
Ravinder.'

Ravinder shook the dice and threw 'five', John moved the counter along *four*
places and proceeded to push it up a ladder. By now an Indian girl had attached
herself to the group.

'No, don't do it for him, let him do it,' she cried.

'He can't, he doesn't know what to do,' John retorted as Michael snatched
Ravinder's counter and pushed it back to square one with the comment 'Ravinder's
not winning'.

Ravinder shook the dice again, he threw 'three' — John began to move the
counter, whereupon Michael stretched out and firmly placing his finger on it,
guided it back to square one.

'No,' protested John.

Michael slid the counter up to square one-hundred.

John persisted in his efforts to see fair play. 'No, put it there.'

Michael moved the counter into the centre of the board.

Ravinder sat and watched.

John and Michael argued.

Ravinder hummed.

'Ravinder — dice.' John threw the dice to Ravinder and it fell on to the floor.

John bent down to retrieve it, but as he could not see it he retired from the
'field' to fetch his spectacles!

John returned, and, with the aid of his spectacles, located the dice and gave it
to Ravinder who had to wait while Michael held the container and blew on to it.

Ravinder sat patiently for two minutes, he then touched John's hair. John
turned away.

Michael tossed the dice container over to Ravinder, who quickly shook the dice
and threw 'four'. 'Four,' shouted John, thwarting Ravinder's efforts to count the
dots; John moved the counter to the top of the board, the dice was shaken and
again it danced to the floor.

The teacher watched Michael and John searching for it. She turned to another English girl. 'Julia, will you show Ravinder how to play snakes and ladders?'

'No, I can't, he doesn't understand what I say.'

John picked up the dice and shook it in the container. Ravinder closed the board. 'No, Ravinder.'

Ravinder took the container from John and shook the dice three times, but he did not look at the number of dots. He blew the dice and then John took it away from him — Ravinder banged the board and John, picking it up, stacked it on to a shelf.

1.45 p.m.

Ravinder held one of the counters between his fingers and tried to flip the other counter along the table — John covered it with his hand. Ravinder glared. 'Shut up,' he shouted.

1.47 p.m.

Ravinder selected some number-matching cards from a box and the teacher walked over to show him what to do; seven children joined her.

Ravinder pieced two cards correctly together. 'Good boy,' commented Julia, who had previously refused to help him play snakes and ladders. The teacher moved away and immediately all the watching children followed her.

2.00 p.m.

Ravinder completed matching the cards and the teacher looked at them. 'You've done those well, Ravinder. Now here is something else.'

She gave him a large peg-board with a tray of pegs. An English boy immediately picked up a peg. 'Come away,' intervened the teacher. The boy moved away, but as he did so Michael began to fit some pegs into the board. Ravinder endeavoured to push him away, but in doing so dropped a peg. He bent down to pick it up and while he did so, Michael removed a group of pegs from the board, and then grasped a handful from the box.

'Shut up,' cried Ravinder as Michael tried to fit his pegs in between Ravinder's. Michael walked away.

2.05 p.m.

The teacher looked at the board and then at Ravinder. 'How many? Count.'

RAVINDER: 'Count.'
TEACHER: 'One, two, three, four.'
The teacher pointed to six pegs. 'How many?'
RAVINDER: 'How many.'
TEACHER: 'Count.'
RAVINDER: 'Count.'
Five children gathered round to watch.
TEACHER: 'Count these.'
RAVINDER: 'Count these.'

The teacher pointed to the pegs.
TEACHER: 'Ravinder, how many?'
RAVINDER: 'How many.'
TEACHER: 'Count them, how many?'
RAVINDER: 'How many.'
TEACHER: 'Come on, count them.'
RAVINDER: 'Count them.'
TEACHER: 'One.'
RAVINDER: 'One, two, three, four.'

Michael stretched across the table and fitted a peg into the board reaching in front of Ravinder. 'Shut up,' pleaded Ravinder, as he steadily pushed a peg into every hole.

Another West Indian boy walked over and 'helped' him cover the board; it was finally completed, a mass of colourful pegs stuck in regimented rows.

2.20 p.m.
'Look what I done,' called out the West Indian boy to the teacher. 'See, look what I done, I done that line for Ravinder.'

The teacher and four children gathered round to appreciate the combined effort. 'Jolly good,' remarked the teacher. She indicated the various colours: 'Blue, yellow, white, orange.' She took Ravinder over to look at the colour chart on the wall and they studied each shade with interest.

While their backs were turned the West Indian boy tipped all the pegs into the box.

2.25 p.m.
Ravinder looked round — he walked over to John and gently touched his face. John stroked Ravinder's face — Ravinder smiled, and returned to the peg-board.

Michael was dropping the remaining pegs into the box. Ravinder grabbed a few odd ones lying on the table and, clutching them in his hand, he walked back to the colour chart and pointed to the colours.

Two English children watched him.

'Oh! I can do *that* — that's easy!' was their only comment.

2.30 p.m.
The children went out to play. Ravinder followed alone.

Playtime
Ravinder made no contact with anyone, and stood throughout playtime with his hands in his pockets.

2.50 p.m.
On returning to the classroom, Ravinder sat quietly on the carpet and listened to a story.

Not another word was said to him or by him until he met his brother

at the gate and together they returned to the security and companion-
ship of their own family to whom words were meaningful and where
they themselves could not only speak and hear, but also understand.

'These immigrant children are no trouble . . . leave them alone and they soon learn
to adjust.' — a headteacher (see p.16).

. . . absolute terms breed violence and hatred. Do the roots of racial prejudice lie
here, in the first futile struggles with an incoherent form of language that will not
permit a sensible resolution of unspoken tensions?
(Eyken 1967, p.42.)

3 The mother tongue

A child who cannot speak English is not a dumb child; he has within himself the heritage of a rich expressive language belonging to his own culture. This language is not just a string of words which automatically becomes obsolete as he ventures across the threshold of the school, it is part of his very being which has developed within him since the first moment when his mother cradled him in her arms and shared with him her own form of speech. Through his mother tongue the child has learnt to communicate, to express his feelings, to reason, to question and to discover — should any teacher bypass such an integral part of his life, unheeding his words simply because she has neither the time nor the understanding to comprehend their message? It is essential that the immigrant or E2L child should be able to express his feelings verbally within the classroom from the first moment he enters school even though his words may not be understood by anyone else. Outlets are imperative for the emotions and anxieties which will arise within himself as he adjusts to the new environment and relationships of school life, and one of the most important and satisfactory outlets is that of speech.

Although it is essential for immigrant and E2L children to learn to speak English as quickly as possible in order to communicate their own thoughts and understand those of other people, it is also important that a balance be maintained between the acquisition of English and the ability to verbalise freely in their mother tongue.

Ego-centric speech

Ego-centric speech is a vital stage in the language development of any young child. It is an essential activity which affects not only his speech but also his cognitive skills.

At the age of five many children continue to use ego-centric speech frequently and the infant teacher is very much aware of the important part this 'thinking aloud' plays in his ability to grasp and internalise new facts as well as in the release of emotions and frustrations. Research has shown, however, that, although the child appears to be talking to himself, his ego-centric speech is affected by what is happening around him, and in many cases it decreases or even stops if a person leaves the room or the immediate environment changes in some way — the link between ego-centric speech and social communicative speech is a very close and strong one. The fact that there is someone nearby who can understand and, if need be, respond to what is being said, does influence the way in which the child chatters although he is apparently oblivious of their presence (Berlyne 1970; Luria and Yudavich 1960; Piaget 1959; Vygotsky 1962; Weir 1962).

Both Piaget and Vygotsky carried out extensive experiments in this field, and because I have found Vygotsky's work particularly relevant to the situations in which non-English speaking children are placed, I feel it is appropriate to include a short extract from a study which he made in 1929.

In our first series of experiments we tried to destroy the illusion of being understood. After measuring the child's coefficient of ego-centric speech in a situation similar to that of Piaget's experiments, we put him into a new situation, either with deaf mute children, or with children speaking a foreign language. In all other respects the set up remained the same. The coefficient of ego-centric speech dropped to zero in the majority of cases, and in the rest to one-eighth of the previous figure on the average. This proves that the illusion of being understood is not a mere epiphenomenon of ego-centric speech, but is functionally connected with it.
(Vygotsky 1962, p.136.)

This experiment has very important implications for the five-year-old children who are admitted into infant schools unable to speak English. What happens to their own natural language development? Does their ego-centric speech dwindle as dramatically as Vygotsky suggests because everyone around them is speaking a 'foreign' language, and, if so, how might their cognitive skills be affected, let alone their language development and the acquisition of English?

I believe it is essential for the young non-English speaking child to be sheltered from as many unnecessary linguistic pressures as possible when he is first admitted to school. This may mean avoiding such situations as group activities which are dominated by the English language of the indigenous children, until he chooses to join them of his own accord.

Ego-centric speech is one major outlet through which a child can express his feelings in his own language. Speaking in this way gives him the opportunity and experience of using his mother tongue in school, of hearing his own voice and even using it loudly! I consider it a vital stage which should be especially nurtured and cherished in the child who cannot speak English.

I was particularly interested during the case-study of Asad to find that although no ego-centric utterances were heard during the observations throughout the first week, he began to make audible remarks during the second week and these gradually increased throughout the term (see p.55). The conversation recorded on pp.72—4 was to me one of the most fascinating experiences I have ever encountered whilst listening to children talking, for it showed that ego-centric speech also plays a very valuable and positive part in the acquisition of the English language.

We realise that young children often rehearse the same word over and over again to themselves (on some occasions for as long as three months according to Piaget) before it is used socially. We also know that they correct their own pronunciation during these solitary 'conversations' and practice different sounds and sentence patterns (Weir 1962). Should we not therefore pay much more attention to the value of ego-centric speech in teaching English as a second language in the infant school?

Socialised speech

The development of children's socialised (or communicative) speech is one of the major undertakings in an infant school. The ability to make ourselves understood by others and to comprehend what others are saying to us is essential to our way of life, but cannot be taken for granted. Verbal communication depends on the common language, and that language may or may not be English.

Socialised speech in Punjabi, Bengali, Italian or any other language is as essential in the community where it is spoken as English is to the indigenous population of Britain, and if a school is serving a community whose common language differs from ours, then that language must have its rightful place and not be considered inferior or superfluous in the school.

The immigrant or E2L child is inevitably referred to as the non-English speaking child. This is a negative and partial description which can so easily be confused with a 'non-speaking' child. Every child has language, but few can appreciate, and many overlook, the immigrant or E2L child's ability to speak fluently.

Of all children who need to socialise well, the child with a dark skin and foreign culture is the one who will require a special ability to speak to others with confidence and grace. This ability has its roots in his early successful attempts to converse socially. The age of four to six years is a critical stage in the development of a child's communicative speech. His ego-centric speech gradually becomes internalised and his socialised speech increases as he reaches out and converses with people beyond his family circle, a step which often requires much reassurance and confidence. But what happens when a child during this period has his efforts to communicate with others crushed beneath the pressure of a completely new and strange set of language patterns, sounds and words?

Extending and enriching the children's language is an integral part of the infant-school curriculum. What happens to the child who spends these crucial years of his life struggling with the bare bones and basic skills of a strange second language instead of developing his natural speech with words of expression and beauty gleaned from new experiences, stories and poetry? Does he ever catch up, or is the joy and richness gone forever?

We cannot expect a child entering the infant school to have a full command of his mother tongue. Some children at this age are still learning to speak in sentences or even phrases, and many have not mastered the correct use of tenses. How often has a young immigrant or E2L child been faced with the task of learning a second language using forms of speech well beyond his own natural stage of development?

When the number of children speaking a common language in one school is large, conversation can take place freely whatever their particular nationality may be. As the children learn to speak English, they use their mother tongue less in the classroom but often revert to it in the playground. In schools where the number of E2L pupils is not high, children can be isolated from those who speak their language and it is important for them to meet together at some time during the day (see p.57).

Teachers have said to me on many occasions, 'I only have one child in my class who cannot speak English, so there is really no problem, he will soon pick it up.' In a school where the number of E2L children is small, the difficulties for the teacher may be less, but the problems encountered by those few children are often more acute, particularly when they are completely isolated by language from all their peers.

In schools where the E2L children are of different nationalities the same isolation can occur. It is so easy for an inexperienced teacher to place together Asian children whose languages differ from each other, or a Spanish, a Greek, a Turkish and an Italian child, and label them as 'non-English speaking', referring to them as 'the group of immigrants'. Each one of these children is verbally isolated from the other and can silently undergo tremendous pressures from those around him. Infant schools with a very small percentage of non-English speaking pupils rarely have any additional qualified staff to help these children; unlike similar cases in the older age groups, they are often left to overcome the language and cultural barriers in the best way they can. The case-study of Suba and Asad indicates some of the frustrations and anxieties with which these children are faced (see pp.57–61).

Children as interpreters

One of the obvious ways to communicate in a multicultural school is to use children as interpreters, but the teacher must appreciate the difficulties and limitations of a five- to seven-year-old.

A teacher asked two seven-year-old Punjabi speaking girls to explain to a new Indian boy that when he heard the bell ring in the playground it was time to come back into the classroom. The girls began to interpret in their own language, but then explained in English that there were no Punjabi words for 'bell' or 'playground'. They were very uncertain as to whether there were such things as 'bells' and 'playgrounds' in India, and assured the teacher that if they did exist they were called 'bells' and 'playgrounds'! The new boy failed to understand. Afterwards a Punjabi speaking adult confirmed that there were words for 'bell' and 'playground' in the Punjabi language, although she adapted her interpretation of 'playground' to 'a ground where you play' — this would not be easy for a child of infant age. If I ask a child in my school to inform a new parent that his boy will need a shoe bag, the interpreter will often use the word 'shoe bag' and find it difficult to select an alternative definition to aid his explanation, e.g. 'a bag in which to keep indoor shoes'. When I describe the article to the child he can then usually translate the meaning for me. (The most satisfactory method, of course, is to have one ready as a visual aid!)

Throughout all my work in multicultural infant schools, the children's equating of language and experience has been noticeable. They infer that if a child is able to perform a particular task or has experienced a certain situation, he will automatically be able to speak about it, and have knowledge of the relevant English vocabulary; likewise, if a child cannot speak about something it is probable in their estimation that he is incapable of doing it.

I was travelling on a coach and sitting next to two Pakistani girls aged seven. Fauzia was fluently bilingual, speaking both Punjabi and English. Nusrat had only recently arrived from Pakistan and had very little knowledge of the English language. We passed an indoor swimming pool and I pointed the building out to Nusrat telling her that it was a 'swimming pool'. Her facial expression indicated that she did not understand, so I asked Fauzia to explain to her what 'swimming pool' meant.

'Oh, she knows,' replied Fauzia.

'I don't think she does.'

'Oh, yes she does, Miss Brown.'

'How do you know she knows?'

'Because she's been there — my Mummy took us last week.'

Turning to Nusrat, who had been intently watching our faces during the conversation, I indicated a swimming movement and endeavoured to make the sound of water.

'That was a swimming pool,' I explained slowly.

'Ah,' she exclaimed, her eyes alight. 'Machine.'

Once again I asked Fauzia to interpret my comment into Punjabi. Finally she agreed.

'I understand,' cried Nusrat, vigorously nodding, and it was obvious that then, and only then, she understood.

Experience and language are interdependent, but one does not guarantee the other. The children find this difficult to grasp. How important it is for adults to appreciate their difficulty and not to make the same mistake themselves (see pp.60–2).

Child–adult dialogue

'The fundamental fact in language development seems to be the nature of the child–adult dialogue.' (Wilkinson 1971, p.103.) Wilkinson was referring to pre-school children when he wrote these words, but the child in the infant school still needs a tremendous amount of stimulation and reinforcement from adults, especially at the stage when he is experimenting with, and developing, his socialised speech (Lewis 1963, 1969; Piaget 1959).

If the dialogue which he attempts in school is in a foreign language that cannot be understood, he immediately loses the stimulation of response and reinforcement to his linguistic efforts. The teacher cannot possibly answer with the same enthusiasm and interest shown to an English child, and, although admiration can be expressed for a piece of work and attempts made to understand the content of the child's communication, a meaningless, one-sided conversation may easily be passed by unheeded. I have overheard more than once the adult response to a young child's comments in his mother tongue, 'Lovely, good, but how do we say it in English?' A boy was asked the name of a particular object, he gave the correct reply in his own language according to my Asian assistant, but the busy teacher working in an overcrowded classroom answered quickly, 'No, it's a . . . ' The English interpretation was automatically given without any further consideration for the child's accurate explanation.

Child—adult dialogue in the mother tongue is a vital factor in the well-balanced development of a child's socialised speech at school, particularly when the language is the one used within the home and family circle. A child's attitude towards his mother tongue can, I believe, be positively influenced when he hears an adult using it effectively within the educational environment of his school, and conversing with that adult adds a new stimulus and dimension to the child's own linguistic achievement (see pp.123—4).

I have known adults who can speak the mother tongue of the E2L children in the school and yet who insist on only using the English language (or, in some cases, who are *only allowed* to use the English language). I am confident that if a child is able, even for a short period, to communicate naturally during the early days in an English school, he will adjust to his new way of life with greater ease, and benefit more than we realise from opportunities of expressing himself in the only form of speech he knows.

Home and school

When trying to estimate the value of adults using the mother tongues of immigrant and E2L children in school, an important aspect to consider is the flow of language between home and school. So much of an infant child's vocabulary before he can read is limited to his personal first-hand experience — or television!

On entering school an immigrant or E2L child will handle materials and participate in activities which are entirely new to him and for which he may have no definition in his own language. He learns the English names but on returning home these will prove meaningless to a non-English speaking parent.

I was having a discussion with a seven-year-old Italian girl who had learnt to speak English in school. 'Carmela,' I asked, 'when you speak to me do you think in English or Italian?' 'When I talk to you I think in English,' she replied, 'but when I talk to Mummy I think in Italian.' She paused, and then smiled, 'But when I do my sums I always have to think in English because we don't do sums in Italian.'

It is natural for a young bilingual child to 'pigeon hole' language according to experience. If, however, a conscious effort is not made to link both languages with the experiences of both cultures, disturbing rifts could easily develop between the non-English speaking parents and their child.

During an outing I watched two Indian children picking bluebells for the first time. The flowers were accidentally left in school and I wondered how the mothers would interpret 'bluebells' in their own language if the children spoke about them at home. Was there a Punjabi word for 'bluebell'? Would the parents have knowledge of it, and would the children be able to describe the flowers sufficiently well for the mothers to understand what they were like and where they came from? The only foolproof way of ensuring complete communication and understanding would be to take the Indian mothers into the woods with the children to pick the bluebells and to discuss the experience in the two relevant languages.

I frequently question the children's activities in this way and always appreciate the help of an adult who can give the child a definition in his own language *during* the experience, or, alternatively, watch an activity and then discuss it afterwards within the family circle, enabling the child to extend the vocabulary of his mother tongue and to communicate fully with his parents (see pp.123—4).

Shared experiences are basic to shared language and when we consider how English children can misconstrue or misplace words in their own mother tongue, I cannot imagine some of the garbled messages and stories which must finally reach the ears of immigrant parents in another language. Only recently an English child told me that he had seen a cockerel revving up its engines during the week-end, and he described the noise with graphic detail! After some questioning I discovered that he was referring to a Comet!

If immigrant adults and parents can share their children's experiences, they should then share their mother tongues with ease, enriching and extending the child's vocabulary with understanding and interest and thus playing an essential and rightful part in their own child's language development (James 1974).

Reluctance to use the mother tongue

From time to time I have had E2L children in the infant school who are reluctant to use their mother tongue with those who speak it once they have mastered English; this applies both to general conversation with their peers and to the role of interpreter. This apparent self-consciousness about their own language gave me much food for thought, and one afternoon my concern was justified.

An Italian mother came to me sobbing. Her seven-year-old son was refusing to speak Italian at home. When she tried to discuss the matter with him he explained that he was English now and he did not want to speak her language. The mother had a very limited understanding of English and she was desperate to know what she could do to prevent this barrier from coming between her and her child. The rift widened and neither our efforts to encourage the child to speak Italian at home, nor our subsequent efforts to give the impression of ignoring his attitude for a while, were successful.

Since that first incident I have had two more Italian mothers with similar problems. Then a few cases filtered through from the Indian community.

A seven-year-old Indian girl was being taken to hospital with a fish bone in her throat. The teacher accompanying her in the ambulance reassured the child by reminding her of all the interesting facts with which she could regale her mother on her return home. 'Oh no,' was the immediate response, 'I can't talk to her, she doesn't speak English.'

One evening I was in my local library searching for literature relevant to the problems facing parents of bilingual children. Unable to find such information I sought the advice of the librarian who happened to be an Indian. When she heard what I was looking for, and why, she shared her own experience with me. Her son, who is now an adult, had learnt to speak English on board ship whilst sailing from

India to Australia when he was six years old. He never spoke again in his own mother tongue, although both his parents and his sister always used it when conversing with him in the home. He understood what they were saying but persistently replied in English. Fortunately both parents and the sister could understand the English language, but the mother has never fully comprehended why her son should react in this way.

I frequently watch Indian children playing in the gardens near to our school, and listen to them chattering away in English. Their mothers and grandmothers sit as onlookers, unable to understand what their own children are saying. It is hard to envisage the divisions caused by language barriers in the family circles of this current gener-ation. How many of these barriers are insurmountable because the mothers cannot understand English and the children will not use their first language?

Could the fact that some children reject their own language be due to a threat in insecurity stemming from the time when they first spoke their mother tongue in school and found it completely inadequate, ignored by adults and despised by other children?

Referring to Labov's work in New York, Wilkinson writes:

Labov suggests that new language habits suffer from interference from the vernacu-lar . . . But much more important, he feels, is the conflict of value systems involved; to accept a language is to accept the values it symbolises . . . 'Identification with the class of people that includes one's friends and family is a powerful factor in explain-ing linguistic behaviour.' In other words, for some children to change one's language is to change one's identity. And this may present such a threat to their security as to be unacceptable; conversely, the individual may feel he would be betraying his family or class by changing.
(Wilkinson 1971, p.98.)

Does the E2L child lose the values which his own language symbolises when he learns to speak English, and does he feel that he is betraying his school, his teachers and his English speaking peers when he uses his own mother tongue? How easy, or how difficult, is it for an immigrant or E2L child to identify himself with two languages and two 'classes' of people?

These are the questions which every infant teacher in a multicultural school should ask, and the awareness of such difficulties should create a sensitivity not only towards the child's development within the English community, but also in his own.

Evidence from other countries . . . suggests that the learning of a second language is improved when the pupil has a thorough knowledge of and ability to use his mother tongue . . . Language is an integral part of both culture and religion and in order for the education system to carry out its responsibility in what is officially recognised as a plural society, the language of minority groups cannot be left to haphazard support.
(Community Relations Committee 1976, p.1. From a CRC letter to the British Home Office.)

4 English as a second language

The most urgent single challenge facing the schools concerned is that of teaching
English to immigrant children . . .

A knowledge of English is essential if the immigrant child is to develop self-
confidence in his new social relationships, to grow culturally in his new environment, to become part of his new community. Inability to speak the language of
the community in which one lives is the first step towards misunderstanding, for
prejudice thrives on lack of communication. If there is any validity in Bernstein's
view that the restricted code of many culturally deprived children may hinder
their ability to develop certain kinds of thinking, it is certainly applicable to non-
English speaking immigrant children who may be suffering, not only from a limi-
tation in a restricted code in their own language, but from the complication of
trying to learn a second language. Experiencing language difficulties, they may be
suffering handicaps which are not conspicuous because they concern the very
structure of thought. It may be that culture shock partially stems from this block-
age in the steady development of concept formation. The bilingual situation can
be a very bewildering one for immigrant children and can produce within them a
sense of psychological and emotional insecurity. It is essential that their command
of English progressively improves so that it is adequate for the increasing demands
made on it and so their real ability does not continue to be masked by language
deficiency while at and after leaving school.
(Department of Education and Science 1971, p.9)

The pre-speaking stage

Before a child can be expected to internalise a new language and use
the vocabulary it is necessary for him to be given time to adjust to
the confusing meaningless jumble of sounds, until gradually he becomes
aware of certain significant groups which occur in the same situations
and are associated with definite patterns of action. This period of listening to, sorting, and differentiating sounds is an all-important first step
in the teaching of English to immigrant and E2L children (see p.107).

It might be better called a learning rather than a teaching phase, for it is a time of
incubation in which the real work goes on unseen and unmeasured in the pupil; his

ears are accustoming themselves to the sounds of a language that fall into patterns — patterns of speech sounds including pitch and rhythmical features — that he has never heard before. He is beginning to recognise these patterns and to respond to them as they emerge from the 'confusion' . . .

The place for commands that involve the pupils in actions . . . and the stage of repeating the teacher's words themselves . . . can only come when the pupils are ready to pass from being simply hearers to being speakers, when language is something which they begin to use actively themselves . . . this moment may be reached in less than a week, or with the very young or nervous pupils it may be after several weeks, and it will not be the same for all the pupils in one group . . .

Finally, we might point out that the process in which pupils begin to respond to any language and obviously understand it before they are ready or able to use it themselves, is one that has a wider reference through all the stages of second language learning. For, in this respect, the second-language learner is like the native speaker of a language who, at any age, has a passive vocabulary which is wider than his active vocabulary.

(Derrick 1966, pp.25–7.)

Emotion and language

For many years now we have been aware of the effect which the emotional state of a child has on his language development, particularly the development of his mother tongue. It can cause him to become completely withdrawn or it may strongly influence the manner in which he expresses himself, the words he selects and the subject matter of his conversation.

The tremendous importance of the close relationship between the emotional state and the language performance of children was impressed upon me very forcibly one day by a West Indian boy aged seven years. Dean was an active boy. He could read simple books steadily and write short but imaginative stories using a reasonably accurate although stilted sentence construction. He conversed freely, and when so doing spoke quickly and with expression, drawing the listener's attention to the content of the conversation rather than to the phraseology and the way in which it was compiled.

On this particular afternoon Dean was very restless and I suggested that he might like to shut himself alone in the vacated secretary's office and make a recording for me. He jumped at the idea, and we quickly set up the microphone and necessary equipment; I left him, suggesting, at his request, that it might be a good idea to begin by recording what he would like to be when he grew up.

After forty-five minutes I returned to the room, knowing that the cassette would have run out. I had heard Dean's voice through the wall becoming louder and louder and when I opened the door I found him hot and sweating, waving his arms about and singing at the top of his voice. That evening I played the recording.

For twenty-five minutes a monotonous, staccato voice related his future ambitions, and then suddenly his intonation completely changed. I listened to the following conversation:

[Staccato and monotonous voice.]
And when it's over for work I'll come back home and I'll get my pay — I'll get how much? Thirteen pounds like my brother used to get when he used to go out on paper round.
I'll go to paper round and I'll go where my brother used to be and I won't get the sack until I leave — Sorry — and then I will get my girl friend a lot of flowers and my girl friend will get me a lot of presents for what I will get for her too.
And when I finish she will finish, and anything what I do, she goes and copies me an' all, and then when she finishes her own self I will finish it my own self —
And we always going to do the same, what each others wants to do, and we will copy and copy and never stop until we go to bed. Amen.
Now here is another one called about so when I grow up I will be another different children and I will be — I will get my girl friend and we will go out a lot a thousand times until one of us sick, and if my sister's still sick with her bad leg and if S—— fight I will tell my Dad and my Dad will have to go down S——'s 'ouse if he touches my sister, because that's what my Dad said you see —
[Change of voice — sing-song intonation.]
So then I would like to do in it — so — when I finish I would like to be a girl and I would like to talk like this in it — then I know
and then I'd be a boy then —
can you see?
Yes.
This would be a very funny joke —
Now sir — yes — this would be very clever.
Right now —
I'd go on a ship — all right!
And if I get kill, I'd die, won' I?
Yeeees —
So then — what's wrong?
Nothing.
Oh yes — very bad indeed —
Oh, oh, no it is not very bad otherwise I'd cry.
You get out of it S—— or I'll kill you . . .
I'm on top of the pops.
[Singing.]
Where's your baby gone, where's your baba gone?
Far far away, far far away . . .

It is not possible to portray in print the change of voice and the difference in tone and expression following 'that's what my Dad said, you see . . . ' After twenty-five minutes of hesitant but deliberate speech, Dean burst forth into excited shouting and singing and he reverted to the intonation of his own dialect. It was as if a new energy had been released and a physical and emotional change had taken place.

Throughout the first section of the tape, Dean appeared to be seeking favour and defending his own position in life. He frequently referred to his 'working in order to buy or give presents to others'; another favourite topic was playing at war games with his gun, when he added 'if anyone tries to kill me, I'll hide.'

Then Dean made his first reference to S——, a boy who had been worrying him, and he expressed both his fears and a solution. 'If S—— fight I will tell my Dad and my Dad will have to go down to S——'s 'ouse . . . ' The tension was released, the boy relaxed and a dramatic change took place in the expression of his thoughts. Not only did the delivery alter, but he became a dominant personality, for example whereas previously he had referred to 'hiding away from death' he now cried,

'If I get kill, I'd die, won' I?
Yeeees —
So then — what's wrong?
Nothing.'

Humour creeps in and then tremendous singing with relaxed rhythm and movement.

Until I listened to the final part of the tape recording I had never heard Dean speaking with a Jamaican accent — he may have used it, but he never used it with me; nor had I been aware of the way he constructed his sentences when speaking. I asked myself to what extent was Dean's language development inhibited not only by the tension within himself, in this case caused by S——, but also the need which he felt to conform as far as he was able to the English way of speaking. How aware of his difficulties was I and how was I helping him?

In a similar way, the emotions and ability to learn a second language are, I believe, interrelated, and it is essential to ensure that E2L children are made to feel as happy and secure as possible immediately they enter school, and before, not after, they have begun to grasp an English vocabulary. Nearly all the children whom I have known to remain silent for months and sometimes years suffering from culture shock,

had been placed in schools where there was no special provision for
language teaching. A few were found in schools where additional help
was given, and in these cases the children benefited from the extra
care and attention which supported and encouraged their efforts to
face and overcome many of their difficulties.

'Picking up' English as a second language

'As there are only a few immigrant children in this school no special arrangements
are made for them. As infants, most of them are able to integrate and pick up the
language quite quickly . . . ' — a head teacher.
(Brittan and Townsend 1972, p.25.)

Many educationalists, as I have already mentioned, are still convinced
that immigrant and E2L children in the infant school are able to 'pick
up' the English language from their peers with ease, and additional
specialised help from adults is unnecessary.

Comments similar to those quoted above are quickly made with little
thought as to how children in an infant school do 'pick up' a language.

My observations show that children in the infant school may have
difficulty in understanding the concept of a different language (see pp.
60—1); if therefore the other children are incapable of placing themselves to a reasonable degree in the position of a non-English speaking
child, are we, as teachers, justified in leaving even one E2L child to
learn English solely by such haphazard methods?

Of course a child will learn a considerable amount of language from
the conversation around him; the indigenous children extend their
vocabularies in this way, and likewise the E2L child, although we must
remember that the latter has no foundation on which to build. However, both the quantity and quality of language acquired by this
'method' are debatable. Is the child with limited English exposed to
a sufficiently rich vocabulary, are the basic phrases and sentence
patterns repeated regularly and correctly, and does he himself practise and use them consistently? How frequently do the indigenous
children converse with a non-English speaking child? Do they listen
with concentrated effort to what he is trying to say and then respond
in a manner which is congenial to further language development? Are
the indigenous children really interested in the progress made by their
non-English speaking peers or do they become bored, or even mysti-
fied, by the persistent lack of verbal response? (See pp.60—2.)

Throughout my teaching experience I have felt more and more that leaving a child to 'pick up' the English language from his peers is unsatisfactory. Not only are valuable language constructions overlooked or omitted, but the children must undergo times of deep perplexity and misunderstanding. One of the main purposes in undertaking the case-study of Suba and Asad was to record not only the words which were spoken by the two boys learning English, but also the vocabulary used by their peers.

The observations revealed some enlightening if disturbing facts: for example, the decrease in the number of remarks made by the children to Suba; the reasoning and conclusions formed by peers in both age groups concerning Suba and Asad's inability to communicate verbally; the contrast between the number of remarks made by the boys to adults and the number made to children; the linguistic dominance of the indigenous children, etc. These aspects highlighted the need for a great deal more time and thought to be given to this haphazard method of learning a new language, especially when so much of the child's education and future career depends on it.

The analysis concerned with the points referred to above is recorded in detail on pp.78–81, and I would ask the reader to study the figures with care and to note their implications.

The view that the study of language need not be designed, but will arise naturally from pupil's observations and questioning (Dixon 1967) leaves a great deal to chance and does not take sufficient account of what little we do know of the learning processes; and, in any case, it makes nonsense of curriculum research and planning, besides placing inordinate responsibility on the teacher . . . (Bradford Infant Centres 1973, p.55. Summary of reports on a Unesco conference held in 1969.)

Withdrawal to a language group

In my experience I have found it essential to have an area in a multicultural school which is set apart for the children who have difficulty in speaking the English language.

The purpose of such a place should not be to sit the children down and drill them in the English vocabulary under the misguided conception, expressed by one of my colleagues in the educational field, that 'these foreign children cannot do anything until they speak our language'.

In the initial stages this area, small though it may be, should enable the children to meet others who speak their own language if at all possible and thus give them the chance to relax and converse freely without the incessant background noise of English. Familiar equipment, which is accessible, provides security for the children, and new activities, introduced slowly and with care, allow time for discovery and the practice of new skills without unnecessary tension, embarrassment and a sense of failure. In this environment the children can share group activities without being dominated or harassed by English speaking children, and a secure and confident base is laid for the foundation of a new second language.

Listening to the children's speech

One of the major advantages of withdrawing children into a small language group is that the teacher has the opportunity to listen to what they are saying, and notice discrepancies which might otherwise pass by unheeded. The mistakes which E2L children make when using the English language frequently differ from those made by the indigenous children; they fall approximately into three categories — pronunciation and phonological discrepancies, grammatical and syntactical discrepancies, and comprehension or semantic discrepancies.

Pronunciation and phonological discrepancies

Children for whom English is a second language will naturally transfer the sounds from their mother tongue to their new form of speech, and often the familiar sounds replace the correct English phonemes — e.g. 'd' replacing 'th' or 'v' replacing 'w'. Special consistent practice is needed to help to correct mispronunciation of words, but before such practice can take place the teacher must be aware of the child's difficulties, and these can only be sensitively isolated when the child is in a small group or alone with the teacher. (See Derrick 1966; Garvie 1976.)

Grammatical and syntactical discrepancies

These discrepancies are frequently overlooked in oral situations, especially in a crowded classroom. Although the tape recording of Dean illustrated discrepancies caused partly by a different dialect, as opposed to those arising from a completely new second language, it was an outstanding example of how we had failed to listen to and notice the way in which a child was expressing himself, because so often we were just concentrating on the content of his conversation — 'And we always going to do the same, what each others wants to do . . . ' Very often we only become aware of the discrepancies in this category when the child begins to write fluently and express himself freely on paper. By then precious time has been wasted, incorrect habits have been formed and sometimes the opportunity to help him has been lost for ever.

Comprehension or semantic discrepancies

These discrepancies in particular differ from those of the indigenous child. They may stem from lack of comprehension, and a misunderstanding of the concept of a word — for example, 'a red' — but very often it is the subtle misuse of vocabulary which, although conveying the correct meaning, is not acceptable — for example, the tea-kettle (tea-pot), the washing string (washing line), a 'bless you' (sneeze).

These mistakes can only be noted in detail and analysed during the comparative quiet of a withdrawal group in a secluded corner or area; the teacher then has both the opportunity and the time to listen (see p.148).

In the withdrawal group a teacher has the time which must be allowed for explaining even a simple assignment to a child who cannot easily understand English. She has time to watch the child, and to listen to his own efforts of speech and communication until she discovers, at least to some degree, what he is trying to say. She can listen to both ego-centric and socialised speech in whatever language the child is using, and thus gain an insight into his development, progress and ability. The teacher dealing with a small group of children has time to talk with them slowly and without interruption. The majority of words expressed in English by Suba and Asad were spoken to adults in a one-to-one relationship, and this has repeatedly been found with many children learning to speak English in our school.

The withdrawn and silent child can be observed carefully to ensure that he is working through a 'listening pre-speaking' period and not suffering from undue culture shock. The child who is undergoing severe problems of adjustment can be comforted and reassured without the clamour of twenty-nine or more other children.

The withdrawal language group is *not* a remedial class. It is sometimes suggested that indigenous children with learning difficulties should be included in this group, particularly those with speech problems or slow immature language development. The needs of these children are quite incompatible with the problems of those learning English as a second language and adjusting to a new culture. The ability of an indigenous child to speak English, even though he may have learning difficulties, is usually far greater than that of the E2L child during the early stages. The former's responses to very basic language patterns can override and silence the E2L child who often needs time to recall a single word or compose, with fumbling effort, a phrase beyond the vocabulary of his own mother tongue. Once English children are included in the language area many of the classroom pressures can creep in and the whole character of the group changes.

The need for qualified and experienced teachers

The importance of the adult's skill and ability to teach English as a second language to children in the infant school cannot be over-emphasised. The following example illustrates the point only too well.

Whilst visiting a multicultural infant school one day, I was told that many of the language problems were solved by well-meaning parents and friends who came into the school on a voluntary basis to give the E2L children some extra help. I was very interested to see and hear how much the children gained from this arrangement, and appreciated the opportunity to listen to the conversation which took place whilst one of the visitors supervised four five-year-old children playing with coloured dominoes in a corner of the classroom. I wrote down the dialogue between the adult and one of the children named Baljit.

ADULT: 'We'll let Baljit start. Put one in the middle.'
She pointed to the centre of the table and Baljit placed a coloured domino in the position indicated.
ADULT: 'Baljit, what colour? Red, say red.'
BALJIT: 'Red.'
The other three children had their turn.
Baljit's second turn.
ADULT: 'Have you a red one?' Baljit nodded.

ADULT: 'Have you a red one?' Baljit nodded.
ADULT: 'Have you a red one?' Baljit nodded.
The adult pointed to the centre of the table, Baljit placed a second red domino in the position indicated.
The other three children had their turn.
The adult pointed to a yellow domino.
ADULT: 'What colour? Yellow — Baljit, say yellow.'
BALJIT: 'Yellow.'
The adult pointed to the green half of the domino.
ADULT: 'What colour? Green — Baljit, say green.'
BALJIT: 'Green.'
ADULT: 'Have you a green one Baljit?'
Baljit pointed to a red one and said 'Yellow.'
The adult pointed to a green one.
ADULT: 'Say green.'
BALJIT: 'Green.'
The adult pointed to each colour in turn.
ADULT: 'Yellow — say yellow.'
BALJIT: 'Yellow.'
ADULT: 'Green — say green.'
BALJIT: 'Green.'
ADULT: 'Red or purple — say purple.'
BALJIT: 'Red or purple.'
Baljit pulled out a red and black domino.
The adult pointed to the black one.
ADULT: 'Baljit, what colour?'
BALJIT: 'Red.'
Baljit banged the dominoes together.
The adult pointed to a blue one.
ADULT: 'What colour?'
BALJIT: 'Yellow.'
The adult pointed to a red one.
ADULT: 'What colour?'
BALJIT: 'Yellow.'
ADULT: 'No, it's red.' She pointed to an orange one. 'What colour, Baljit?'
BALJIT: 'Yellow.'
ADULT: 'No, orange.' She pointed to a blue one. 'What colour, Baljit?'
BALJIT: 'Yellow.'
ADULT: 'No, blue.'
BALJIT: 'Blue.'
The adult pointed to an orange one.
ADULT: 'What colour?'
BALJIT: 'Yellow.'
ADULT: 'Not yellow.'
BALJIT: 'Yellow.'
ADULT: 'What colour? — orange,' she pointed.

'What colour? — mauve,' she pointed.
'What colour? — red,' she pointed.
BALJIT: 'Yellow.'
Baljit stood up and left the table.
ADULT: 'Where are you going, Baljit?'
Baljit went and fetched a piece of painting paper — he painted a yellow face!

Many young indigenous children in the infant school find difficulty in
recognising and naming colours, but Baljit could quickly sort and match
them as I discovered later. The adult's lack of experience, initiative and
technique caused the child to become confused and bored. Her speech
was very quick, she hardly every paused and her voice sounded monotonous. Although at first she asked Baljit to repeat the names of the
colours she should have encouraged him to use phrases such as 'It is
red' or 'It's a red one'. As the game continued she failed to give Baljit
the opportunity to rectify his own mistakes and reinforce the correct
answers — for example when he called the black domino 'red' and the
blue one 'yellow' his answers were ignored, and when he called the red
domino 'yellow' he was briefly told that it was 'red' but not given a
chance to repeat 'it's a red one' — the adult immediately pointed to an
orange one and continued in this fashion. It appeared that she was
fearful of losing the children's interest which is not surprising. I had
longed to take Baljit away from the dominoes that morning, and
wander around the school with him, discovering together the articles
of one colour only and concentrating on the name and language
patterns connected with that specific colour.

This one example is typical of some conversations which I overhear
between adults and young non-English speaking children. When visitors
and students spend time in our school I am always interested in the
way they speak to the E2L children. I have often noticed an adult rue-
fully leave a child, uncertain as to how his well-meaning but rather one-
sided conversation became so distorted! It is not easy to maintain a
flow of conversation which is neither too complicated nor too simple,
nor ambiguous to the young child who cannot understand English.
Colleagues who assure me that they have no problems with their E2L
children who apparently 'pick up' English without difficulty cannot
always suitably adapt their conversation to the needs of the Asian
children whom they meet in our school; this may be due to the fact
that their experience is often with older children and in many ways
it is harder to communicate and adjust adult language to the younger
age groups, particularly when they cannot speak English. Specialised

experienced adult help is essential in this work at the infant stage.

I cannot over-emphasise the need for *active* language teaching. When students and, occasionally, other professional colleagues assist us with the E2L children, they so often gravitate towards books, and the conversation dwindles to a session of brief questions and answers. Referring to a picture the children are asked 'What is this?' and, if the correct name is given they turn to another illustration with the same question, and so the routine continues. We must move away from some of our own memories of second language learning and *live* the English language with these children if we want them to learn it successfully and well. (See chapter 11.)

It is important to bear in mind the range of responses which a word can evoke. Take, for example, a young child learning the word 'pretty'. He discovers its meaning through seeing and touching a wide variety of attractive articles to which he can respond with delight, thus he slowly grasps the wholeness of its concept. In a similar way the young child learning English as a second language must also have opportunities to experience the different associations with certain words in order to understand and appreciate their meaning thoroughly (see p.145). In so doing he learns not only to use the English vocabulary, but also to experience and understand the depth and richness of the language and the culture it represents. As June Derrick writes, 'teaching language does not consist of simply teaching words any more than learning a language consists of just words' (Derrick 1966, p.6). Language habitually channels thought according to the choice, selection and use of words available, and the child in the infant school is not 'acquiring the words of a second language in order to solely communicate with others at school, he is living and working through that language which permeates the whole of his reasoning powers, his thought processes and his emotions' (Whorf 1966).

Education authorities should do everything possible to enable teachers in multicultural schools to become aware of the techniques and skills required to teach a second language, and this applies to infant teachers as much as it does to those working with older children. A person who is qualified to teach reading and extend the language of an indigenous child is not automatically equipped for teaching English as a second language. Teachers cannot necessarily 'pick up' such skills any more than the children can be expected to 'pick up' the language; nor should the class teacher be expected to carry out such a task with twenty or thirty other children in the room all seeking and requiring her attention.

Teachers talk of teaching language in the infant school, but what is really meant is that the teacher expands, develops and enriches the vast amount of language that the British five year old already knows. The assumption that the immigrant child will be able to absorb by some process of osmosis all the previous English language experience that the British child has acquired in five years is surely demanding the impossible.

The language work which normally takes place in an infant school is for the most part inappropriate for immigrant children.

(Schools Council Working Paper 31, 1970, p.42.)

PART TWO

Closer observation – Suba and Asad

The case-study

This study concerns two brothers, Suba aged 6½ years, and Asad aged 5½ years. The children arrived in England from Bangladesh with their parents and two older brothers. The father and brothers had a limited command of English, the mother had none. The family spoke Bengali and, according to our observations and efforts to communicate, neither of the younger children had any understanding of English when they were admitted to school, apart from Suba's ability to count 1 to 30 in rote fashion. It was thought by the headteacher that Suba possibly had associations with a playgroup or something similar in Bangladesh, but neither of the boys had regularly attended school.

Suba was placed in a class of twenty-two six- to seven-year-olds, and Asad in the reception class consisting of thirty-four children — no one spoke their language although the children were of several nationalities.

During the observations, particular attention was given to situations in which any form of communication was indicated and they were classified under six headings as follows:

(1) Suba and Asad's verbal expression using the Bengali language.
(2) Suba and Asad's verbal expression using the English language.
(3) Remarks made by other children either directly to or about Suba and Asad.
(4) Remarks made by adults either directly to or about Suba and Asad.
(5) Physical contact between Suba or Asad and other children.
(6) Physical contact between Suba or Asad and adults.

Observations were made throughout the first week and on Tuesdays and Thursdays until the completion of the term. The days were numbered according to the boys' attendance in school, i.e. week-ends and days of absence were not counted.

The first section of the case-study was made during the three weeks immediately following the boys' admission to school. In order to watch the boys in as many different situations as possible, I switched frequently from room to room and the length of time spent in each observation varied considerably.

During weeks 1 to 3, Suba was observed in the classroom for 10 hours 30 minutes, and Asad for 15 hours 20 minutes. Additional observations were made during the cloakroom, playground and lunch time activities.

The second section of the case-study was made during weeks 4 to 12 when each boy was observed in the classroom for a complete day every week. An equal length of time (27 hours) was spent with each child, thereby enabling a fairer comparison to be made.

Throughout the case-study, Suba was observed in the classroom for 37 hours 30 minutes and Asad for 42 hours 20 minutes.

Although the scope of these observations is narrow — only two children were observed for a very short time — the findings strongly supported hypotheses suggested by a much wider personal experience.

5 Use of the mother tongue

Ego-centric speech

The first analysis concerned the ego-centric speech of Suba and Asad in their mother tongue, Bengali. Suba made 7 audible utterances and Asad more than 52 during the observations (see fig.1).

Suba's ego-centric speech ceased completely after week 7. Because of his age we could assume that he was reasonably competent in the use of his own language and past the stage of excessive audible ego-centric speech. It is not surprising therefore that the utterances were few in number and decreased until they were non-existent. The teacher responsible for a non-English speaking six- to seven-year-old child should bear this in mind and look for alternative ways to encourage or give opportunity for the child to express himself verbally during his first weeks in school (see pp.123—4). Suba spent hours sitting silently.

Asad's ego-centric speech was restrained during his first weeks in school, but after he had begun to speak in the second week it gradually increased and was frequently interspersed with humming, singing or whistling. Asad appeared to use ego-centric speech when he was sitting alone, but contented and concentrating with interest on a specific task.

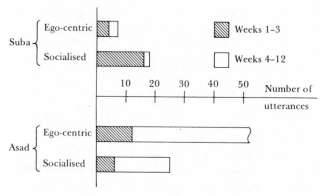

Fig. 1. Analysis of utterances in the mother tongue

It was occasionally difficult to differentiate between the Bengali and English words during the latter weeks, and Asad's combination of the two languages was fascinating to hear, particularly on day 37 week 9 (see p.72). The uninhibited, natural ability of Asad to speak aloud in this way, and his need and desire to do so, helped him to practise and master new words and the phonemes required to speak the English language.

Socialised speech

The second analysis concerned the socialised speech of Suba and Asad in their own language. Suba made 18 socialised utterances in Bengali during the observations and Asad made 25 (see fig.1).

The majority of Suba's socialised utterances occurred whilst he was trying to communicate with other children in 'shared' activities. Owing to the tremendous difficulties of comprehension it appeared that Suba only expressed himself when he was either dressed in costume clothing other than his own enabling him to take on the role of another person, or when he was in a state of emotional tension and insecurity. The need for Suba to communicate with his peers appeared to be greater than Asad's because whereas Asad seemed to be content to play on his own or alongside another child (a natural stage of development for his age group), Suba tried desperately to communicate with the others (see pp.57–9).

During the observations made in the classroom, Suba spoke his mother tongue in what appeared to be a relaxed manner on only one occasion, when he smiled at a hat which a child was wearing and made a comment to the child concerned. Only two utterances in the mother tongue were recorded after week 7.

The majority of Asad's socialised utterances in Bengali were made whilst he was trying to communicate in a one-to-one relationship with an adult who spoke only English. The circumstances were congenial and Asad expressed himself with apparent ease. The utterances used in connection with children, however, were made on occasions of frustration giving rise to a defensive attitude.

Unlike Suba, Asad continued to use his mother tongue in both ego-centric speech and socialised speech with adults throughout the whole of the term. Indeed, his speech in Bengali increased.

Conversations between Suba and Asad in school

The situation in which Suba and Asad were placed was one where
nobody spoke their language and the two boys never met or communicated in any way during school hours. Occasionally they caught
a glimpse of each other in the hall during the morning assembly, but
their classrooms were separated by a long corridor, and they played
in separate playgrounds and ate their dinners at different sittings.

The following extract from the case-study shows what happened
when a special arrangement was made for the two brothers to meet.
(These observations were not included in the analyses as they were
made outside the normal class activities.)

On four occasions I brought Suba and Asad together in one of the classrooms and
listened to their conversation as they wandered freely round with each other.

The first occasion was on day 4 — Friday afternoon at the end of their first
week. The transformation which took place, particularly with Asad, was astound-
ing. The Bengali conversation which flowed from the boys, who until then had
been almost silent, tumbled forth endlessly in excited tones and exclamations
accompanied by expressions of happiness and joy which I had never seen before.
The whole physical attitude of their bodies and the ways in which they moved
were suddenly revitalised as they spoke and shared together their experiences,
giving each other the confidence to experiment, to touch and to discover.

On day 6 the conversation between the boys was not so continuous and it
decreased even more on day 8 although they both enjoyed playing with the
equipment in the classroom together. It appeared that the first expressions of
delight had gone, and instead they showed their appreciation of each other's
company in a quieter and more contented manner.

On day 16 (week 4) the boys were again brought together but on this occasion neither of them spoke. It was their only opportunity of discussing their
school activities with anyone within the building but they remained silent . . .
As far as I am aware they never shared another conversation in their own
language during the whole of the term, and they were unable to communicate
with anyone else.

Frustrations and difficulties

The following extracts from the case-study of Suba illustrate the
child's frustration and difficulties during co-operative play because
socialised speech was impossible.

Day 1.
Suba walked over to Narinder who was working with clay and plasticine; he

tapped her on the shoulder, but she gave a shrug and continued with her work.

Narinder left her model, wandered over to the shop, and stood by the till. Suba followed her almost immediately but he was pushed away. 'No,' she cried. Suba argued in Bengali, Narinder in Punjabi — neither understanding a word of what the other was saying.

Suba poured some sweets into the weighing pan and then tipped them back into the jar. He placed some weights on to the scales and again poured out the fruit drops making a colourful heap. Narinder grabbed the pan and emptied the sweets back into the jar. Suba began to play with the till, he pressed the keys and watched the cash drawer spring open, then he filled the drawer with weights; Narinder looked at him, her eyes wide. 'They're weights not money, you mustn't play with that.' Suba turned sharply and accidentally knocked a large sweet jar which wobbled and descended with a crash. He bent down to retrieve it and his elbow poked the ice-cream 'cornets', they too toppled to the ground — tenderly Suba picked them up one by one . . .

The scattered items were finally returned to the counter and Suba walked over to Narinder and clutched her shoulder — she shook him away. 'Oh wait a minute,' she sighed, and then paused, 'Oh all right, come on.'

She tugged his sleeve and pulled him over to where some children were playing snakes and ladders. Suba picked up the dice and vigorously shook it in the container, he threw it on to the carpet with a smile — but, as he did not have a counter and no one could explain the rules, the other children took the dice and ignoring him, continued with their game.

Suba sat in a chair and watched.

Day 2.

Suba wandered round the classroom apparently looking for something. He went to a pile of books and lifted them up one by one as if seeking his own — it was not there. The children began to lead out for dinner. Suba ran over to Narinder and tugged her arm. She would not move and pulled her arm away. Suba ran to another pile of books and glanced through them but could not see his own.

The children were disappearing through the door, Suba followed . . . Where was his book?

Suba was playing behind the sweet shop. He snatched the till from an English child. Having played with it for a minute he put it down, and pushing past another child went over to a third English child — he appeared to want the sweets she was holding and twisted her wrist in order to get them. The child scowled at him. 'Don't do that,' she cried, at which one of the onlookers retorted, 'You mustn't be rude to him — he's only just come to school, he's new.'

Day 3. Playing in the home corner

Suba suddenly stretched out and caught hold of Barry's spectacles — he was smiling.

BARRY (shouting): 'Don't, you're not allowed to touch my glasses — they mustn't come off.'

Barry clutched his spectacles, he pulled them away from Suba and put them on again.

Suba picked up a mirror, he looked into it and then, stretching out his hands, once more removed Barry's spectacles. He held them in front of the mirror casting a bright reflection on to the wall.

BARRY: 'Don't.'

Suba tried on the spectacles, and looking into the mirror, smiled, then calmly handed them back to their owner.

Suddenly Suba caught hold of Barry and pulled him along the corridor and then back into the home corner. He slammed the door.

BARRY: 'It's cold, it's cold.'

Suba put on a cap and, speaking in the Bengali language, looked into the mirror.

BARRY: 'Give me that hat.'

Suba made no response — Barry pulled it off.

Suba lashed out and caught hold of the cap. Barry tugged it until finally Suba let go. Suba unhooked a satchel from a peg, Barry snatched it away and hung it on his back.

Suba spoke in his own Bengali language with an angry intonation.

BARRY: 'No, I want it.'

Suba spoke to Barry in Bengali — there was no response from Barry. Suba pulled a scarf from Barry's neck and twisted it around his own. He turned and snatched off Barry's spectacles again.

BARRY: 'No, you mustn't.'

Suba carefully balanced the spectacles on his nose, and then returned them to Barry with a smile. He picked up the postman's cap and placed it on his head speaking to Barry in Bengali.

BARRY: 'I can only think in English.'

Suba spoke again in Bengali and removed the cap. Barry muttered his own imitation of Suba's speech.

RITA: 'Let's go inside.'

BARRY: 'Yes, let's pack up, (to Suba) PACK UP.'

Suba spoke in Bengali, he replaced the cap on his head, and, speaking Bengali, took Barry's hand (obviously trying to say 'Come').

BARRY: 'No, I'm going to pack up.'

Suba hung the satchel on his back, and marched up and down the corridor. He turned, and, walking back to Barry, stretched out his hands.

BARRY: 'Oh no, not my glasses again.'

He hid his face . . . Suba punched him.

Reactions of peers

During my study of Suba and Asad careful observations were made concerning the reaction of other children in the class towards the boys' Bengali speech, and the conclusions to which they accordingly arrived.

Extract (a). Day 8. Week 2.

I asked two of the Punjabi speaking childrein in the class whether they could understand what Suba was saying when he spoke Bengali.

'No, of course not, *he can't talk.*'

'Oh yes he can,' I replied, 'You listen, we can hear him speaking on my tape recorder.' I played the recording and the girls laughed when they heard their own voices, then Suba spoke in Bengali — the children paused.

'*That's not talking,*' they said.

During the observations on day 8 when the above conversation took place, the Punjabi/English speaking children were reasonably confident that Suba understood their instructions. 'I think he understands but *he doesn't know how to do it . . .* I'll do it for you.' To them it appeared that Suba's inability to speak their language and respond to their verbal information signified that he was incapable of performing the task in hand.

If these *bilingual* children were unable to appreciate Suba's problems, how much more difficult it must be for an indigenous child to realise the help which Suba needed.

Extract (b).

On the first day Helen, who had been instructed to look after Suba by another child, did her utmost to draw out a verbal response from him.

HELEN: 'Do you want to play a puzzle with me?
Do you want to play a puzzle with me?
[Slowly.] Do you want to play a puzzle with me?
Say "yes".'
SUBA: 'Yes.'
HELEN: 'At least he said "yes". Put the lid on. [She pointed to the lid of the box.] Put the lid on.
He's Indian, I'm English.
He can do it, look.
Put the lid on.'
Suba responded.

Extract (c).

Some of the English children were aware of their own frustration arising from their inability to communicate with Suba. It was in an exhausted tone of voice that Barry remarked after dinner on the second day, '*He keeps talking to me in Indian and I don't know what he's saying.*' On the following morning as Barry listened to Suba's Bengali comments in the home corner he cried '*I can only think in English*' and then made an attempt at his own gibberish version of Bengali which had no resemblance to the language whatsoever and consequently brought no response! (See p.59.)

Extract (d). Day 16. Week 4.
Stephen and Asad were playing with water.

> STEPHEN: 'That's better, I've filled up with petrol. Oh, I've got a lot of petrol.
> D'you like playing with water, Asad?
> D'you like playing with water, Asad, eh?
> D'you like playing with water, Asad?
> Shall I help you? Can you hear me, eh?
> Poor Asad, *he can't hear.*'

Extract (e).
> INDIGENOUS CHILD: 'Asad's being a nuisance — he keeps hitting us — *can he talk?*'

Extract (f). Day 44. Week 10.
Stephen and Asad were playing in the home corner.

> STEPHEN: 'Asad, get the cups out please, Asad.
> All these cups out Asad please.
> Get all these cups out Asad.
> *Can you see, Asad?*'

Extract (a) illustrates the fact that a bilingual child who is aged seven years and has the personal experience of learning a second language still cannot necessarily appreciate the full concept of 'a different language' when it applies to another child. The Punjabi/English speaking children failed to recognise Suba's speech as a means of conversing, and even made the assumption that he could not talk. In extract (c) Barry appeared to be trying to make Suba understand when he spoke in his own gibberish.

These children recognised that Asian children speak differently, but they could not fully grasp that the noises which Suba made was a structured, expressive language, as meaningful as their own when used in a Bengali community.

The children aged five in examples (d), (e) and (f) inferred from Asad's inability to understand that he was deaf, dumb and, at one point, possibly blind.

During the study it was obvious that the English speaking children equated the inability to speak with the inability to achieve (extracts (a) and (b)). The fact that Suba and Asad were unable to partake fully in certain activities because of their lack of communication, implied that they were completely incapable of doing so. In example (a) the children had no reason to believe that Suba had understood what they had said. He had not understood, and he showed no indication whatsoever of comprehending their Punjabi interpretation of the teacher's suggestion to draw what they had seen on the television programme. The comments, attitudes and actions of the English speaking children in both classes indicated that Suba and Asad were, in their estimation, less able than themselves. The following comments recorded in the case-study reinforce this.

Suba's peers
'Making a pattern? Good — very good!'

'Shall I make a sun for you?
[The child drew on Suba's illustration.]
. . . There we are. Look, that's nice.
There's a star and there's a sun.'

'Now, I'll take your apron off.'

In the home corner.
'I'm going to read you a story.
Suba, sit here, you won't see the pictures.
· · · Suba, come and sit here. Sit here.'

Asad's peers
Undressing for PE.
'Asad hasn't taken his trousers off.
Can't he take them off?'

In the home corner.
'Asad, get these cups out please, Asad.
. . . Good boy, Asad.
Now the saucepan.
. . . Good boy, Asad; that's a good try.'

Conclusions

(1) It is essential for non-English speaking children to spend time with an adult in a one-to-one relationship or in a small group.
(2) Communication with English speaking children is difficult and can place a considerable strain on the non-English speaking child, creating a variety of problems.
(3) The seven-year-old child requires urgent help to enable him to speak English as quickly as possible because:

(a) he wishes to communicate with his peers;

(b) the decrease in Suba's use of his mother tongue indicates that he would remain silent, unable to express his thoughts, until he mastered the English language.

Why did Suba stop speaking his own language?

(a) He possibly restricted his comments in Bengali realising that they were not understood by either the teacher or his peers.

(b) The observations indicate that he was concentrating on listening to, and learning, English.

(c) The children and Suba shared in fewer group activities as the term progressed — once Suba understood what was expected of him he preferred to work alone and independently.

(d) The English speaking children could not appreciate or respond to Suba's comments, and they tired of his speech, becoming almost antagonistic towards it on occasions.

(e) The number of remarks which the children made to Suba showed a considerable decrease throughout the term, and therefore necessitated fewer comments and replies from Suba.

(f) Due to lack of understanding there was little response to Suba's comments and no linguistic feedback from adults in the school.

Has the analysis of socialised utterances made by Suba in Bengali any relevance to the inhibitions which some children experience towards speaking in their mother tongue? (a) and (b) are inevitable in the circumstances in which Suba was placed, (c) could depend on the child's personality, but (d), (e) and (f) could have an important bearing on the problem of disowning or despising one's mother tongue.

6 Use of the English language

Suba

We have seen from the observations of Suba that the needs of an older child to learn English appear, in certain respects, to be more urgent than those of a younger child (pp.55, 70). The needs of an immigrant or E2L child who is admitted as a single newcomer into an established group of children are also very different from those of a child of five who is admitted alongside other children to school for the first time.

Apart from the desire to communicate with the adults and his peers, a child aged six to seven years has a thirst for knowledge and is usually anxious to read and write alongside the other children in his class. It is very likely that he is under pressure from his parents to acquire these basic skills as well and as quickly as possible and he may already have mastered to a certain degree the equivalent skills in his own language. Efforts to help him to adjust and learn English should be made as carefully and as promptly as possible.

In the previous chapter we looked at the occasions on which Suba spoke his own language; let us now refer to the number of English words he used and the situations in which they were spoken during the observations, remembering that he was placed in a normal class without being given any additional specialised help.

Apart from counting, Suba independently recalled and spoke a total of 385 English words (113 different); 334 (88 different) were spoken to adults and 51 (25 different) to children. An additional 92 words (67 different) were repeated but not memorised — 88 after adults and 4 (on the first day only) after children.

The words Suba used with adults

The words are placed under the day on which they were first heard. The figures indicate the number of times the word was spoken throughout the observations. Words marked with an asterisk were read from cards or a reading book.

Day 1. Week 1. (Nil.)
Day 2. Week 1. (Counting 1 to 31.)
Day 3. Week 1. (Counting 1 to 5.)
Day 4. Week 1. Bag (1), bed (1), boat (1), cup (4), fruit (1), hand (1), jug (1).
Day 11. Week 3. Cap (1), dog (7), mug (1), sun (2).
Day 13. Week 3. (Nil.)
Day 18. Week 4. And (3), apple (2), ball (4), balloon (4), banana (3), bath (4), biscuits (3), brush (3), bus (4), car (4), cat (7), chair (3), chocolate (2), comb (3), doll (5), fish (5), flowers (3), gloves (2), house (3), Jane* (24), moon (1), orange (6), pencil (2), Peter* (8), shoes (4), sock (2), spoon (3), sweets (4), tap (3), teddy (4), telephone (3), television (4).
Day 21. Week 5. A* (2), here* (9), is* (11), likes* (1).
Day 31. Week 7. Bicycle (2), book (2), clock (1), Dick* (17), donkey (1), eyes (1), funny* (5), glasses (2), jump* (2), look* (25), mouth (1), nose (1), oh* (30), pear (1), potatoes (2), Puff* (3), Sally* (7), see* (26), Spot* (2), tea-pot (1), tree (1), water* (1).
Day 37. Week 9. Egg (1), grass (1), horse (1), paper (1), milk (1), swing (1), tomatoes (1), window (1).
Day 43. Week 10. Chicken (1), onions (1), swan (1).
Day 50. Week 12. Barry (1), boy (2), do (1), doing (1), E— (1), Leslie (2), Mrs (1), Tony (1).

Apart from 'brush and comb' spoken on day 18, and 'here is a' and 'oh see funny Sally' read on days 21 and 31, Suba did not use any phraseology with adults during the observations until day 50 when he said quite spontaneously, 'Mrs E— boy doing. Look boy do.' It is important to note that natural phraseology was introduced only when Suba spoke spontaneously to adults for the first time.

Spontaneous conversation arising out of activities and experiences shared by an adult and a non-English speaking child plays a major part in helping the child to learn the English language, particularly if the adult is acutely aware of the language structure being used, and has the necessary skill and knowledge to seize or make opportunities for introducing and consolidating a controlled foundation of language patterns (Garvie 1976; City of Bradford Metropolitan Council 1978).

The significant factor which emerged from the analysis of the words Suba spoke in English was the difference between the number of words spoken to adults and the number spoken to children. Suba spoke nearly six times as many words to adults as he did to or with children, and the majority of his speech occurred during a one-to-one

relationship with an adult or whilst working in a small group supervised by an adult.

Once again we return to the fundamental importance of child—
adult dialogue (Wilkinson 1971), but, in Suba's experience, there
were very serious limitations. The words which he used with adults
consisted of a list of disjointed nouns, labelling disconnected objects.
This was partially due to his early stage in the learning of English, but
the stilted vocabulary was also a direct result of the content and
phraseology of the conversation with adults.

Suba's strong desire to read and his quick visual memory enabled
him to recognise and remember symbols with comparative ease. During his fourth week he was recognising and saying the words 'Jane'
and 'Peter', and by the seventh week he could recognise and say
'here', 'is', 'a', 'look', 'Dick', 'Oh see funny Sally', 'Puff jump', 'water'
using cards without the aid of illustrations. This for him was a satisfying
achievement because he was proving himself to be as able as the other
children in the class and his efforts evoked praise from the adults. It
is essential, however, for every teacher to remember that recognising
and naming printed symbols is not necessarily reading with understanding (see pp.114—15).

The words Suba used with other children

Day 1. Week 1. No (1).
Day 2. Week 1. (Nil.)
Day 3. Week 1. (Nil.)
Day 4. Week 1. Come on (6).
Day 11. Week 3. Helicopter (1).
Day 13. Week 3. Yes (10).
Day 18. Week 4. Shut up (6).
Day 21. Week 5. Car (1), Peter (1), shur-off (1).
Day 31. Week 7. Good morning (1), hip-hip-hooray (1), lighthouse (1), shut off (1).
Day 37. Week 9. Barry (2), get off (3), hello (on the telephone, 4), Tony (1).
Day 43. Week 10. Ball (1), horses (1).
Day 50. Week 12. Blue (1), green (1), leader (1), me (1), orange (1), toilet (2),
white (1).

The small vocabulary which Suba learnt from and used with his peers,
was meaningful and relevant to him. He was able to apply the words
to a situation and use them to express his thoughts and communicate
his feelings. This was in contrast with the larger vocabulary used with
adults which was just a string of nouns.

Some of the terms used were colloquial and grammatically incorrect, but they belonged to his peer group and were therefore clearly understood and accepted by the children.

Although Suba was probably unaware of the fact, he coupled words together from the fourth day onwards as he 'picked up' such phrases as 'come on', or 'shut up'. Suba's first efforts to link words purposefully and voice them aloud were made during the twelfth week, when he said 'toilet — yes — toilet?' and 'me leader'. There was very little repetition and consolidation in the limited vocabulary which Suba used apart from 'come on' and 'shut up', and the sentence patterns were haphazard.

The majority of occasions on which Suba spoke were emotional ones, involving other children during general class activities. 'Shut up', 'shut off' and 'get off' were uttered when children interfered with the activity in which Suba was personally engaged at the time.

Summary

The first word which Suba spoke in English was 'No!' This was uttered on the first day to a child who tried to push him away from the shop till. It was the only English word recorded on day 1. Suba had learnt to count to over thirty in English before attending school. He first showed this ability whilst working with an adult on the second day.

It was not possible to discern from the study alone how essential it is for a seven-year-old to have the experience or complete understanding of a word before he can remember it. However, when comparing the words which Suba remembered with those he failed to recollect, the importance of the child basing his new vocabulary on a meaningful concept is significant and emphasises the need to involve, as far as possible, practical experience, emotion and personal understanding. Whilst looking through a picture book Suba was told the name of each article illustrated. Later he remembered 'bed', 'bag', 'jug', and 'cap' — these were objects with which he had played in the home corner. He was unable to recall 'wig', 'top' and 'nut', which was not surprising!

Both Suba and Asad remembered and verbalised with ease 'boat', 'car', 'helicopter' and 'dog'. Their tone of voice in these instances was one of interest, indicating that the whole concept of the words was appreciated through personal first-hand experience. The other major advantage, which teachers should be aware of, is the likelihood of words such as these having been incorporated on previous occasions in the boys' own language. If a list of the words common to both English and the first language could be compiled, it would surely be a helpful starting point casting light in the child's confused darkness of muddled communication.

Asad

Apart from counting, Asad independently recalled and spoke 208 English words (80 different); 204 (77 different) were spoken to adults and only 4 (3 different) to children. An additional 108 words (73 different) were repeated but not memorised. All these were repeated after an adult, none after children.

The words Asad used with adults

Day 2. Week 1. Bo (boat, 4), car (8), dog (14).
Day 3. Week 1. (Nil.)
Day 4. Week 1. Donkey (4).
Day 8. Week 2. Cock-a-doodle-doo (cockerel, 1), ears (2), eyes (5), mouth (2), toilet (5), window (2).
Day 11. Week 3. Ass (donkey, 1), flowers (5), scissors (4), tractor (2).
Day 13. Week 3. (Nil.)
Day 16. Week 4. Apple (3), biscuit (2), bread (1), clock (2), cup (5), doll (5), orange (6), red (3), teeth (2), yellow (11).
Day 21. Week 5. Baby (1), cake (3), horse (2), rabbit (2), tree (5).
Day 31. Week 7. Ball (5), banana (1), basket (1), bath (1), bed (3), book (2), bricks (1), brush (2), bus (1), cat (2), chair (2), cot (1), hand (2), house (6), shoe (5), sweets (1), tongue (1), train (5).
Day 37. Week 9. Boy (3), cap (2), elephant (1), fish (6), gloves (1), helicopter (1), kettle (1), keys (1), lollipop (1), milk (1), oh (1), sun (1), table (1), teddy-bear (4), telephone (2), television (1), tomatoes (1).
Day 42. Week 10. Blue (2), green (5), lighthouse (2), plane (2), white (2).
Day 50. Week 12. Chicken (1), gun (1), Mrs (1), P— (1), pear (1), teacher (1), umbrella (1), yes (1).

The words Asad used with other children

Asad was not heard speaking to other children until day 42 week 10. Like Suba, the first word he used was 'no'. The other words were 'thank you' (1) and 'fish' (2); both were spoken on day 50 week 12.

Because of his age and stage of development, Asad did not show any strong desire to communicate verbally with his peers, and they, in turn, rarely interfered with his activities, the majority of the children being engaged in parallel play.

Summary

During weeks 1–3 all the English words, apart from 'toilet', spoken by Asad were the names of objects learnt in a one-to-one relationship with an adult, and not one English word was spoken directly to a child until week 10.

The significant factor of the *whole* analysis was again the difference in the number of words spoken to adults and the number spoken to children (204:4).

The words which Asad remembered were ones for which, I believe, he had a personal underlying concept; unless one has lived in the area it is sometimes difficult to appreciate the concepts within the experience of a five-year-old child from another part of the world. The only phrase which Asad was heard to use throughout the observations was 'Yes Mrs P—' during the register on day 50 week 12.

7 Aspects of second language development

The need for a five-year-old to learn English is probably not as urgent as that of the seven-year-old because:

(1) at this particular stage of development children often prefer *individual or parallel* play to social group play.
(2) it was observed that Asad's *ego-centric speech* increased, enabling him to express his feelings verbally to a certain degree.
(3) the *children's remarks* to Asad increased instead of decreasing as in the case of Suba.

It should also be noted that much of the equipment in the classroom could be used without language; therefore, with a little extra assistance in the beginning, Asad was able to occupy himself alongside the other children.

Now let us probe further into these three points. So far we have used them in a rather negative way as valid reasons for lessening the urgency of a five-year-old child to learn English immediately he enters school; but, have they a positive contribution to make in actually helping him to master the skills required in order to speak the English language?

Parallel play

I was watching and listening to two five-year-old children in Asad's class sitting next to each other at a table, both occupied with a puzzle; one was an Indian, the other a West Indian.

> The Indian child turned to the West Indian and spoke in Punjabi.
> The West Indian 'replied' in English 'Can't you do it?'
> The Indian child 'answered' in Punjabi.
> The West Indian responded with 'He doesn't know how to do it' and continued with his activity.

Two different children in Asad's class were sitting at the 'junk' table making individual models. Again one was an Indian, the other a West Indian.

> WEST INDIAN CHILD: 'What are you doing?'
> The Indian child 'replied' in Punjabi.
> WEST INDIAN CHILD: 'Can you move over?'
> The Indian child 'replied' in Punjabi.
> The West Indian child put a brush into the paste jar beside the Indian child.
> The Indian child spoke in Punjabi.
> WEST INDIAN CHILD: 'All right!'

These children could not speak or understand the other child's language. The interesting point was that each child was able to express his thoughts in his own words without being verbally rebuffed by the other, and with no apparent concern about his peer's unintelligible response. He was only really interested in his own comment and, although in the first example the English speaking child drew his own conclusions regarding the inability of the Indian child (which in this case might have been valid), he made no effort to either help or hinder him.

This attitude, which was evident amongst the five-year-olds and is even more prevalent in my nursery class, allows the non-English speaking child to carry on a conversation in his own language without any derogatory comments from his peers, and indicates that he is not unduly perturbed if they respond in another language.

The speech in the above examples was ego-centric to a certain degree, but it was used in a definite social context. The children could hear each other's language even though they did not appear to listen to it, and all these comments were made during a relaxed, absorbing activity.

Ego-centric speech

We now study two examples of Asad's ego-centric speech.

Day 21. Week 5.
Asad was sitting alone clipping unifix cubes together.
> 'Bengali speech . . .
> Fifteen, fifteen.
> Say thank you.
> Bengali speech . . .
> Bengali speech . . .

    Seven.
    Humming.
    Bengali speech . . .'
Asad tipped the cubes back into the box.
    'Five.'

In this example Asad was transferring from one language to another in a natural rhythmical pattern, incorporating words and phrases which he had heard in the conversation around him.

Five minutes before the following ego-centric conversation the teacher and I had both noticed and remarked on the conscious effort which Asad had to make in order to twist his tongue round the English pronunciation of numbers when counting.

Day 37. Week 9. 11.27 a.m.
    'Eighteen, nineteen, twenty.
    Eleven, twelve, thirteen, fourteen, twenty.
    Twenty-one, twenty.
    Twelve, twenty.
    Twelve, twenty.
    Twelve, twenty.
    One, two, three.
    Humming.'
Asad pulled out some cubes and then put them away again; returning to the squares he laid them out one by one.
    'Three, four, five, six.
    Twenty, twenty-eight, twenty-nine, twenty.
    Twenty. ⎤
    Twenty. ⎟   [Each one was sung in an
    Twenty. ⎟   interval of a third.]
    Twenty. ⎦
    Bengali (muttered).
    Thirteen.
    Seventeen.
    Eighteen.
    Twenty.
    Twenty-five.
    Twenty-six. [Asad picked up the squares.]
    Twenty-seven.
    Humming.
    De-dee.
    De-da.
    Thirteen.
    Fifteen.
    Seventeen.
    One, two, three, four.
    Three, four.

Three, four.
Three, four.
Br, br.
Br, br.
Brg, brg.
Nineteen, nineteen.
Twenty, twenty.
Twenty-one, twenty-one.
Twenty, twenty.
Twenty-one, twenty-one.
De-rr, de-rr.
Three, three.
Ter-rr; terr-rr.
Trr-ain; tr-ain.
Te-rr; te-rr.
Three, three, three.
Bengali.'
ENGLISH CHILD: 'Look.' Asad ignored her and continued with his ego-centric speech.
'Te-rr; te-rr.
Twenty-one, one.'
TEACHER, speaking to another child: 'Very good.'
ASAD (ego-centric speech continued):
'Verry-good, verry-good. [Pause.]
Verry good.
Verry, very.
Vr, vr.
Two, three; two, three.
Bengali.
Two, three, four, five. [Packing up squares.]
Twenty-one, twenty-two.
Two, three, four, five. [Laying out squares.]
Two, three, four, five.
Oo-oo; oo-oo.
Two, three, four, five.
Humming.
Uugh.
Twenty; twenty-two. [Asad placed cubes in a row.]
Twenty; twenty-two.
De-dee; de-dear.
Humming.
De-dee; de-dear.
Humming.
De-dee; de-dee.
Nineteen, twenty.
Nineteen, twenty.'
Asad stood up. He pushed past Kamaljit.
TEACHER: 'All right, Asad?'

Asad continued to walk purposefully towards the mathematics area. He picked up a box of dominoes, and holding them carefully returned to his table.

He silently laid out the dominoes, then, when the row was completed, he hummed.

'De-dee; de-dee.
Bengali.
La-la; la-la. [Asad piled up the dominoes.]
De-dee; de-dee.
De-mee; de-mee.[He made up a second pile.]
Dor-ren; do-ren. [Louder.]
DOR-REN; DO-REN.
DOR-REN; DOR-EN-O.
DOR-EN-O; DOR-EN-O.
DOR-EN-O; DOR-EN-O.
DOR-EN-O; DOR-WIN-O.
DOR-WIN-O; DOR-WIN-O.
DOR-WIN-O.'

11.46 a.m.

TEACHER: 'Children, pack up'.

Asad pushed the dominoes into the box, returned them to the mathematics area and walked to the teacher saying softly to himself: 'Dorwenno, dorwenno, dorwenno'.

TEACHER: 'Sit down.'
ASAD: 'Toilet?'
TEACHER: 'Yes.' Asad went . . .

Asad's efforts to recall and master the word 'domino' were not prompted or helped in any way by another person. I did not hear the word used by anyone on that day prior to this example of Asad's ego-centric speech.

Not only was Asad's ego-centric speech allowing him to express himself verbally, he was internalising and recalling English words and phrases, practising pronunciation and the mastery of new phonemes, becoming accustomed to voicing aloud the English language, and enjoying the sing-song rhythm and intonation of new speech patterns.

Ego-centric speech plays a vital part in a young child's acquisition of a second language, and, as stressed in chapter 5, the nursery and reception class teacher should ensure that a child is happy and secure, in circumstances which will encourage ego-centric speech.

Children's remarks to Suba and Asad

We left our non-English speaking children in the free atmosphere of the classroom and let the other children teach them . . . ' — a head teacher.
(Brittan and Townsend 1972, p.25.)

If we leave children in the infant school to learn the English language from their peers, we must have some knowledge of the words that are spoken to them. The non-English speaking child can only grasp the vocabulary he hears.

Because this is such an important issue I am going to refer in detail to the analysis of the remarks made by children to Suba and Asad during the observations in the case-study. How frequently did the children speak to Suba and Asad? What vocabulary did they use and how and why did they use it?

The following extracts from the study are examples of a five-year-old's speech to Asad on three occasions.

Day 16. Week 4
Stephen and Asad were playing beside each other at the water trolley.
STEPHEN (turning to Asad): 'Look at this . . .
     I'm filling up with petrol.
     Do you like this warm water?
     Do you like this warm water?
     Do you like this warm water?
     Do you like this warm water, Asad?
[Louder.] Asad, do you like this warm water?
     Um?
[Pause — no response.]
     It's nearly filled.
     I'm filling up with petrol, Asad.
     Here's the petrol.
     That's better. I've filled up with petrol.
     Oh! I've got a lot of petrol.'
A child passed by.
CHILD: I'll come and play with you sometime.
     I'll come and play with you Stephen and Asad.'
The child walked away.
STEPHEN: 'D'you like playing with water, Asad?
     D'you like playing with water, Asad, eh?
     D'you like playing with water, Asad?'
The child passed by again.
CHILD: 'I'll come and play with you.'
The child walked away.
STEPHEN: (to Asad): 'Shall I help you?
     Can you hear me, eh?
     Poor Asad, he can't hear.
     He's taken my petrol.
     I want my petrol.
     I want my petrol.
     I've got a lot of petrol in here.
     I've got a lot more petrol left.

I've got a lot more petrol left . . .
Asad, are you playing anymore?
Asad, are you playing anymore?
Do you like playing in the water, Asad?

Day 42. Week 10.
In the cloakroom.
JOANNE: 'Open your mouth.
Open your mouth, Asad.
Wide. [Joanne held up her fingers opening them widely.]
Open your mouth.
Open your mouth.
Open your mouth *wide*, Asad. [Held up fingers.]
Open your mouth.
Open your mouth.
Open your mouth.
Open your mouth *wide*, Asad. [Held up fingers.]
Wide. [Joanne held up her fingers, Asad held up his.]
Wide.' [Joanne held up her fingers. Asad held up his again.]

Day 44. Week 10
Steven walked over to Asad.
STEVEN: 'Let's play in the wendy house.'
The two boys entered the home corner.
'Will you get the dinner ready, Asad?
Will you get the tea ready, Asad?
Go on, Asad.'
Asad was handed the tea-pot.
'Asad, get the cups out please, Asad.
All these cups out, Asad, please.
Get all these cups out, Asad.
Can you see, Asad?'
Asad was handed a pile of cups and saucers.
'Good boy, Asad.
Now the saucepan.'
Asad passed two saucepans to Steven.
'No, only one, Asad.
Good boy, Asad, that's a good try.
No more, Asad.
Good boy, Asad.
Get the dinner, Asad.
Now you sort the dinner out, Asad.
Do you like playing in the wendy house, Asad?'
Asad lifted the telephone receiver to his ear.
'Ring your own Mummy up, Asad.'

Steven placed a blanket around Asad's shoulders. Asad ran to the teacher and
Steven followed.

     'Asad put all the things out . . . '

Asad entered the home corner and laid out four saucers. Steven put his arm
round him.

     'Asad sit down.'

Steven pulled Asad on to the floor.

     'Asad, you play with us, you play with us.
     [To children outside.] You can't come in, Asad's playing here.
     You can't come in, Asad's playing here.
     Asad, do you want a dress?
     Would you like a dress?
     Do you want a dress?
     Do you want a dress?
     Do you want a nice dress, Asad?
     Here is a dress, Asad.
     This is gorgeous Asad.
     Good boy, Asad.
     That is gorgeous, Asad.'

Steven held up a voluminous flowing skirt.

     'Put your feet in, Asad.
     Put your feet in, Asad.
     This is gorgeous, Asad.
     Put your feet in, Asad.'

Steven tried to push Asad into the skirt.

ASAD: 'No.'

STEVEN: 'Asad, you're a good boy.
     Asad, you're a good boy.
     Asad is a good boy in the wendy house.'

These examples clearly illustrate the dominating aspect of a five-year-
old child's conversation, and also his doubt concerning Asad's hearing
and sight. But they also emphasise two extremely valuable and important contributions which a five-year-old's speech can make towards
helping a non-English speaking child to learn the second language:
(1) the repetition of words and phrases;
(2) the rhythm and regularity of speech patterns.

    The five-year-old is still reinforcing and practising his own mother
tongue and in doing this both he and the non-English speaking child
benefit from such a natural exercise — providing the dominating
aspect is kept under reasonable control!

Let us now analyse the *type* of remarks the children made to or about Suba and Asad. Their remarks were placed into nine categories as follows:

Dominating — commands given by children, e.g. 'Come here'.
Critical and reprimanding remarks, e.g. 'Don't do that, you mustn't'.
Approving — remarks of approval, e.g. 'Good boy'.
Outgoing remarks — those which indicate sharing, helpful remarks, e.g. 'I'll come and play with you'.
Explanatory remarks — efforts to interpret or explain something, e.g. 'I'll show you how to do it' or 'This is a dog'.
Questions — interrogative remarks.
Personal remarks — those made to another person concerning Suba or Asad, e.g. 'I think he understands'.
General statement — general remarks connected with Suba or Asad, e.g. 'Suba's gone out to play'.
Self-centred — remarks made by a child to Suba or Asad concerning his own interest, e.g. 'Look what I've done'.

The number of remarks in each category is given in the table and plotted in fig. 2.

	Weeks 1—3		Weeks 4—12		Total	
	Suba	Asad	Suba	Asad	Suba	Asad
Dominating	41	8	8	45	49	53
Critical	7	3	10	25	17	28
Approving	4	0	3	9	7	9
Outgoing	10	2	2	4	12	6
Explanatory	37	4	14	1	51	5
Questions	11	1	7	30	18	31
Personal	5	3	12	3	17	6
General	2	0	4	10	6	10
Self-centred	14	4	4	18	18	22
Total	131	25	64	145	195	170

Suba

Children made 195 remarks to or about Suba throughout the observations. Significantly, the number of remarks made during the obser-

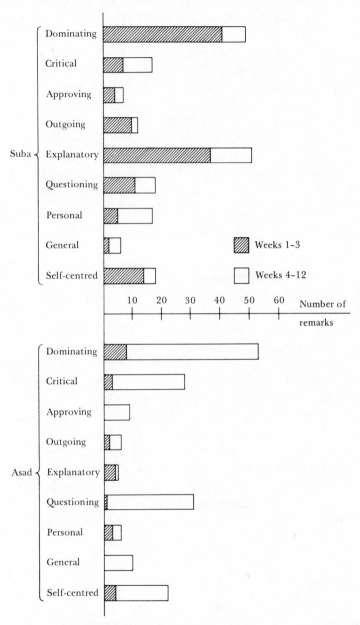

Fig. 2. Analysis of children's remarks to or about Suba and Asad

vations of weeks 4—12 (64 in 27 hours) was less than half the total of the first three weeks (131 in 10½); it was, moreover, the same as the number spoken within two hours of Suba's arrival on the first day. The frequency of explanatory remarks (the category with the highest total) decreased as dramatically, with 22 made in two hours on the first day, 37 during the observations of weeks 1—3, and 14 during weeks 4—12.

There were periods lasting two to three hours when no child spoke to Suba. These were during the more formal activities, although the English speaking children conversed freely all the time. The majority of the children's remarks to Suba were made during group activities; those voiced when he was trying to read or write often imitated the teacher.

Asad

During the observations 170 remarks were made by children to or about Asad; 25 of these were made during the first three weeks, and 145 during weeks 4—12.

In weeks 1—3, the majority of children working near to Asad were engaged in parallel play and ego-centric speech. They appeared to ignore Asad and he in turn ignored them. The remarks by the children were made during different activities at varying times during the day — none of these activities involved groups of children engaged with Asad in co-operative play, but *there were no remarks of approval.*

The number of remarks increased in weeks 4—12, but it is important to note, however, that 107 of the 145 remarks were spoken by the same child during two long conversations — one partially ego-centric, and the other very dominating (see pp.75—7). However, it must be remembered that the natural conversation of a five-year-old often consists of dominant remarks due to his stage of language development (Templin 1957).

Comparison — Suba and Asad

The most significant factors arising from the analysis were:
(1) the high number of dominating and critical remarks compared with
    the low number of explanatory, outgoing and approving remarks
    (excluding the first day in Suba's observations);

(2) the difference in the total number of remarks for each boy, and the
reversal in the totals for weeks 1—3 and weeks 4—12.

This analysis concerns only two children, and they were brothers
in the same school. Is it right to generalise on such narrow, individual
evidence — how many of the children's attitudes and remarks were
affected by the personalities of Suba and Asad, and should we draw
conclusions from such a limited source?

This particular piece of research was carried out in order to con-
firm what I had observed during the course of many years prior to
the study, whilst watching children and listening to their conversations
in multicultural infant schools. As a practising teacher it was impossible
to record what I heard, but I became very much aware of the weight
and content of verbal communication between English and non-English
speaking children in this particular age group. Having worked on the
case-study of Suba and Asad, I am even more aware of dialogues
between non-English speaking children and their peers, and repeatedly
the conversations which are heard in my school today, particularly
between the Asian and the indigenous children, have similar conno-
tations to those I was able to record in detail and analyse.

'Picking up' English

Summary

The language which the non-English speaking child learns from his
peers has a quality of its own. The vocabulary is selected and used by
the E2L child himself; the words are those which he finds he needs and
not those which an adult thinks he ought to know. The vocabulary is
socially accepted by the children, and meaningful and vital to the
E2L child's requirements when relating to his peers. It is a living
language which has been learnt through communication arising from,
and during, shared active experiences.

The non-English speaking child will 'pick up' language from his
peers, but he learns it in a haphazard colloquial form according to his
own needs, emotions and desire to communicate. He can only grasp
the words he hears, i.e. the words the indigenous child *uses;* the fund
of language which remains in the English speaking child's passive
vocabulary will never reach the E2L child.

It appears from this study that it is easier for a five-year-old or younger child to 'pick up' a second language than it is for a child aged six to seven years or older.

Conclusions

We cannot presume that children in the infant school are necessarily able or willing to explain or teach something to, or interpret for, a child with a very limited English vocabulary; they lack the sustained patience and interest required to do this. They become frustrated at not being able to communicate with their non-English speaking peers (signs of frustration with Suba occurred as early as the second day) and aggressive physical contact can be caused by this frustration. Children tire of trying to converse with someone who cannot speak their language, particularly in the older age group, and there can be long periods when no one even makes an effort to talk to the non-English speaking child.

Children in the infant school tend to be critical, and, because of their own stage of development, give little praise or reassurance to their non-English speaking peers. They also tend to be linguistically dominating towards them.

It is difficult for children in the infant school to have an objective understanding of the needs of a non-English speaking child, and give him the necessary constructive help he needs. They may attribute his failure to respond to the idea that he is incapable of carrying out a particular task, rather than the fact that he is merely unable to understand the verbal instructions.

English speaking children in the infant school may not be able to appreciate or understand the concept of 'a language' — i.e. 'being able to speak another language but not being able to speak or understand English' — and so may not comprehend that the seemingly incoherent sounds made by a non-English speaking child are those of a language with the same potential of meaning and communication as their own. The remarks of the indigenous children in the study — 'he can't talk', 'he can't hear' — indicated an inability to grasp the situation fully both from their own point of view and that of Suba and Asad.

Although an E2L child will learn a considerable amount of valuable language from other children, we should never entirely leave him to 'pick up' English from his peers and hope that they will 'teach' him. Additional skilled adult supervision and teaching is essential if an

E2L child in the infant school is to master the English language successfully and with comparative ease.

Adults' remarks to Suba and Asad

There are two analyses of the remarks which adults made to or about
Suba and Asad. Although allowances must be made for the adults'
individual personalities, the analyses do make us aware of certain pit-
falls which might be avoided.

Adults made 245 remarks to or about Suba throughout the observations, 37 during weeks 1–3 and 208 in weeks 4–12. The remarks
to or about Asad totalled 369, with 91 being made in weeks 1–3 and
278 in weeks 4–12.

The first analysis divided the remarks into eight categories:

	Suba	*Asad*
Commands	57	93
Questions	68	103
Explanations	43	78
Approval	37	39
Criticism	3	29
Remarks through other children	21	2
General statements	14	22
Replies	2	3
Total	245	369

This showed the following.
(1) The categories with the highest remarks to both Suba and Asad
    were those containing questions. Questions can be ambiguous to
    a non-English speaking child and require an answer using a dif-
    ferent arrangement in the language structure or intonation. This
    is something which a child must learn, but it is not easy during
    the very early stages of second language learning. (Derrick, 1966,
    does not introduce questions until Step 4, Stage 1 in her book
    'Teaching English to Immigrants'.) In the normal course of child–
    adult communication in the infant school, questions play an essen-
    tial part and should be one of the most common forms of speech.
(2) The difference in the totals of the number of remarks 'made
    through other children' (i.e. interpreting or additional explanation)
    emphasises the ability to use and involve other children in the

older age group. This is one major advantage which multicultural junior, middle or senior schools have over infant schools.

The second analysis calculated the proportion of remarks supported by a visual representation of their meaning, either through objects, actions and gestures or physical contact. It showed that 147 of the 245 remarks to Suba and 254 of the 369 to Asad were supported in this way. This means that 40% of the adults' remarks to Suba and 31% of those to Asad were without any visual representation and so would appear ambiguous or meaningless to the non-English speaking children.

8 Physical aspects

Physical contact with children

During the observations 295 physical contacts were made between Suba and his peers, 137 were initiated by Suba and 158 by other children. 97 of these contacts were aggressive, 43 instigated by Suba and 54 by other children.

245 physical contacts were made between Asad and his peers during the observations, 119 were initiated by Asad and 126 by other children. 97 of the contacts were aggressive, 53 instigated by Asad and 44 by other children.

The detailed analysis is given in the table.

	Suba	Asad
Congenial contacts	49	53
Defensive contacts	22	27
Contacts replacing words	51	28
Contacts involving objects	76	40
Aggressive contacts	97	97
Total	295	245

In both cases the number of aggressive contacts was very much higher than those in other categories. This frequently appeared to be due to language frustration. The congenial contacts with Asad were nearly all made when holding hands with a partner in a line leading to or from the classroom.

Physical contact with adults

During the observations 54 physical contacts were made between Suba and adults and 119 between Asad and adults.

The detailed analysis was as follows:

	Suba	Asad
Reassuring contacts	0	17
Assisting contacts	0	9
Demonstrating contacts	42	49
Correcting contacts	2	8
Contacts made by child	10	36
Total	54	119

It is interesting to see the difference between the number of contacts made with each boy. Note also that there were no reassuring or assisting physical contacts with Suba, probably because he was older.

Perceptual-motor skills

The following extracts from the case-study illustrate the difficulties and frustrations of Suba and Asad concerning perceptual-motor skills.

Day 1. Week 1.
An English child and Suba tipped the puzzle pieces out of a box; they scattered across the table. Suba was not able to fit any of them together correctly — he placed the shapes into meaningless positions. The English child continued successfully to interlock the sections and complete the picture . . .

Suba stood up, he walked over to the shop, he watched the children playing — he slowly strolled round the classroom with his hands in his pockets . . .

Day 4. Week 1.
Asad watched a child successfully complete the puzzle which he had previously attempted. He lifted it up and looked underneath. He dropped a piece of puzzle on to the table and smiled — this action was repeated eight times . . .

Asad picked out pieces of felt from the 'fuzzy felt' box, he tried to fix them together like a jig-saw puzzle. (This was not successful.) He poured them back into the box and placed the board on top. He walked away.

The difficulties were probably caused by the cultural mismatch of home and school.

Day 21. Week 5.
Suba picked up a writing card with words and pictures. He held it upside down and studied it carefully.

Suba laid the card upside down beside his writing book.

He copied the pictures in detail and coloured them exactly as they were illustrated on the card. There was a purple sock, a brown spade, a slide and a stool. Suba copied all of them upside down.

He then turned to a second card. Again he looked at it upside down and drew several sticks of candy floss standing on their heads!

Day 37. Week 9.
Suba laid his picture book on the table upside down. He turned to the illustration of a ball (clearly lying on a floor which was reversed) and copied 'll ᵉ q'.

Day 49. Week 12.
The teacher reported that Suba had copied four dogs from a card upside down with their feet in the air.

Day 11. Week 3.
Asad looked at a picture book which was placed sideways on the table in front of him. He turned the pages over towards him and softly whispered in Bengali.

Day 21. Week 5
Asad pulled out a large picture book — he turned the pages slowly over one by one and looked at them carefully — the book was upside down.

Day 42. Week 10.
Asad took a book from the shelf — it contained many colourful illustrations of footballers. Each page was studied with care although the book was upside down.

Some indigenous children in the infant school, especially those in the reception class, look at books in this way, and the above examples may simply indicate the immaturity of Suba and Asad. Both these boys, however, proved to be intelligent and quick to learn. They enjoyed handling books and were observant; they also had previous experience of literature in the script of their own language. Their difficulty of positioning the printed pages correctly stemmed, I believe, from their inability to re-orientate their perceptual-motor skills quickly to the reading material in the classroom.

Discovery without words

The ability to learn is still within the reach of a child who cannot understand or speak the language of the teacher. The following phrases selected from the observations of Asad during the first three weeks show how he was making simple but basic discoveries without the use of words.

Day 2. Week 1.
Asad *watched* her face all the time.
> He *touched* the plasticine.
> He *watched* a child go to the teacher to have his coat fastened.
> He sat by his peg and *watched*.
> He *watched* the children raising their hands.
> He *watched* the headmistress who had entered the classroom.
> He undid a nut with a spanner and *blew* on a screw.
> He *balanced* a pile of plastic squares on its side.

Day 3. Week 1.
Asad watched.
> No response from Asad . . . he just *watched*.
> Asad *followed* . . .

Day 4. Week 1.
He watched a child successfully complete the puzzle which he had previously
attempted. He *lifted it up and looked underneath*.
> He *dropped* a piece of puzzle on the table and smiled, *he repeated this action
eight times*.
> He *banged* . . .
> He *looked* . . .
> He *touched* . . .
> He *copied* . . .
> He *tapped* his fingers on the chair in time to the music, he *listened*.
> He picked out the pieces of felt and *tried* to fix them together like a jig-saw
puzzle. (This was not successful).
> He *poured* them back into the box and placed the board on top.
> He fitted interlocking shapes *together* and then *pulled* them *apart*.
> He *held* the soft material *to his cheek*.
> He *held* the hard plastic fish *to his face*.

Day 8. Week 2.
He *balanced* some cones and some pegs.
> He *sniffed* and *blew* on the various materials in the Mathematics area.
> He *matched* the colours.
> He *sorted* the shapes.
> He went to the washroom and *tried* each tap in turn.
> He *shut* the classroom door, opened it, and closed it again.
> He *blew* on a brick.
> He *turned* the wheels of a car.
> He *drew* some squiggles . . .
> He *stroked* a West Indian child's hair.
> He sat *shutting* his eyes and *opening* them, he blinked hard and continued doing
so until he realised the children were moving — he ran after them.
> He *balanced* cylinders and *counted* beads.
> He *balanced* some dominoes, then selecting one, he *stroked* it down his cheek.

He *washed* his hands. He put in the plug and *filled* the basin, then *pulled* out the plug and let the water run away. (*This was repeated three times.*)

He moved to another basin and went through the same procedure.

Day 11. Week 3.

He *wound* up a clockwork dog and *watched* it move.

Day 13. Week 3.

He *filled* a beaker with water and *poured* it through a funnel, he *squeezed* a plastic bottle and watched some water squirt out.

He *lifted* a gallon container filled with water.

He *pressed* an empty bottle into the water — it bobbed up.

He *tipped* the water from his beaker through an English child's funnel — there was no comment from either child.

He *splashed* water.

He *flicked* water.

He *blew* at a Lego model.

He separated the layers of a tissue handkerchief, and *folded* one layer into four quarters.

He *balanced* some bottle tops.

He *swung* on the ropes.

He *climbed* on the apparatus.

He *flicked* the door handle up and down as he made a final exit!

These actions, simple though they be, show how Asad was quietly experimenting and discovering the new environment for himself. He was given time to adjust without undue pressures from the teacher, his peers and his own personal standards of achievement.

9 Conclusions

Supportive aspects of Asad's classroom and age group

The fact that it has often been said that 'the infant non-English speaker picks up English by virtue of being an infant in an infant school along with English-speaking children' (Schools Council Working Paper 31, 1970) is partly due to the advantages of being a five-year-old in the *reception* class of an infant school. Asad appeared to have more advantages than Suba because he was in this situation.

(1) The experience and understanding of *all* five-year-olds is limited because of their age, therefore the explanations and requests in the reception class are more likely to be presented in a simple direct form, often supported by a visual aid.

(2) The regular routine in the reception class gave Asad security, whereas Suba appeared sometimes to find the independent movement of older children confusing.

(3) The basic apparatus and equipment in the reception class could be used by a non-English speaking child, and, although Asad needed assistance and encouragement in order to piece together certain manipulative apparatus, there were a few indigenous five-year-olds who needed similar help.

(4) It was necessary and essential for the reception class teacher to give time for educating children in general basic behaviour at school, e.g. how to use the toilet, how to care for equipment, when to walk and when to run in the building. The general organisation of the classroom was sensitively but definitely teacher directed, especially at such times as milk distribution or moving from the classroom into the cloakroom and out into the playground. Asad benefited greatly from the teacher's instruction in these areas, whereas Suba had to notice continually what the other children were doing and try to copy their behaviour which was not always an ideal example!

(5) The reception class teacher gave time to the little details which

have usually become automatic to a seven-year-old child, e.g. how to turn over a page, how to hold a pencil. Both Suba and Asad needed this guidance.

(6) The pace in the reception class was slower. I do not mean the length of the activities, but the allowance of time for packing up, lining up, dressing in the cloakroom, preparing to go to the hall, etc. The seven-year-olds, being more independent, were inclined to rush at everything, often leaving Suba one step behind, whereas Asad was able to keep up with the pace of the five-year-olds and benefited from repeatedly being told what to do.

(7) The relationship between the teacher and the children in the reception class was more demonstrative — facial expressions, the tone of voice and the movement of hands, the assistance given to the children when dressing or putting on aprons, and the reassuring hand clasps, were far more prevalent with the adults and children in the reception class than they were in the older class.

(8) Asad, and also many of the other children in the reception class, devoted a considerable proportion of their time to parallel play when there was no need or desire to communicate verbally with any other child. This lack of involvement in co-operative play eased the pressure which is imposed upon a non-English speaking child during situations involving a considerable amount of language. Suba was frequently caught up in the natural group activities of the seven-year-olds, and they often proved very demanding for both him and the children with whom he was trying to play and converse.

(9) Asad's ego-centric speech increased as he became more confident, and relaxed in his own activities, and gradually English words were introduced into his Bengali repertoire — these were repeated, and so were the new English phonemes. Thus uninhibited, he was helping himself to master new sounds.

A seven-year-old child's audible ego-centric speech has normally decreased, and, apart from counting, Suba was never heard repeating English words to himself.

(10) In the reception class there appeared to be more situations in which Asad could succeed or even excel amongst the five-year-old children, e.g. fastening coat buttons, distributing milk. Suba, however, found difficulty in competing with the capabilities of the seven-year-olds (and I am not of course referring to compari-

son in intelligence). In the reception class there appeared to be fewer situations which necessitated a command of English, e.g. Asad could sort cubes or thread beads without any verbal explanation, whereas Suba was faced with measuring equipment and assignment cards which required a certain amount of language.

(11) The basic vocabulary of a five-year-old is less than a seven-year-old and the sentence formation is often simpler. The rhythm and repetition of a five-year-old's speech could possibly be of more help to a non-English speaking child than the more complex, sophisticated speech of a seven-year-old.

Advantages of Suba's age group.

(1) The teacher was able to use and involve other children in helping Suba. If they had spoken his language they would also have been capable of interpreting.
(2) Provided that he understands what to do, a seven-year-old is able to concentrate for longer periods of time.
(3) A seven-year-old should have a more mature mastery and understanding of his own mother tongue, and, therefore, require fewer opportunities involving experience and practical situations in order for him to comprehend and appreciate the concepts of new English words and sentences. (This does not mean that such experiences should be altogether omitted.)

N.B. These supportive aspects would also be incorporated in the work of a language withdrawal class.

The time factor

How long does it take for a child left in the infant class to learn English as a second language?

In a congenial environment the majority of immigrant and E2L children in the infant school adapt to their new surroundings and learn to use a simple English vocabulary with incredible speed, but of course their progress depends on many factors, the major ones being the ability of each individual child and the home background. I remember a six-year-old Turkish boy (and his parents) who learnt to speak, read and write English satisfactorily after one term, but in the same class a Turkish girl remained silent and moved on to the junior school without having uttered a world of English throughout the whole year.

When a child appears to have happily integrated within the class, and have a sufficient command of English to communicate his immediate needs and requirements, a teacher should *never* assume that the pupil can speak the second language fluently. Children can be great deceivers, and some may continue for years in school with only a limited English vocabulary containing the words they require in order to 'get by'. In these cases little further language development and extension takes place unless the teacher is aware of the difficulty, and not only do the children encounter tremendous problems at a later stage when trying to cope with specific subjects such as Science, History or Geography, but their whole thought and learning processes can be confused and limited (Bernstein 1958; Whorf 1966).

In *Immigrant Children in Infant Schools* we read:

Many of the teachers consulted in the course of the survey said that in the 'normal' class situation the non-English speaking children learn English simply by picking it up, and *can speak it within three months of their arrival*.
(Schools Council Working Paper 31, 1970, p.27.)

Referring to this claim, Mrs Stoker (on whose report the working paper is based) writes:

The term 'to speak English' was, however, highly subjective and in many cases was found to mean that the child had picked up enough words to get by in the school situation.
(*Idem.*)

Mrs Stoker emphasised the necessity for teachers to become aware of the high priority which must be given to structural patterns in language learning, and the way in which these may be taught deliberately or incidentally.

Very many immigrant children who pass from infant schools into junior schools go straight into the language class if one exists. The high incidence of such cases refutes the whole notion that non-English speaking children pick up an adequate knowledge of English in the infant school.
(*Ibid.* p.28)

In *Organisation in Multiracial Schools* we read:

A number of headteachers wrote that infants placed in a normal class would quickly pick up English, but these headteachers tended to be in schools with lower proportions of pupils with weak English. For example:

'Our non-English speakers have been one Pakistani, one Israeli, one Chinese and two Italians. We left these children in the free atmosphere of the classroom and let the other children teach them. *All these children understood what was said by the end of the 1st term,* began to reply and write sometime during the second term'.

'Entrants (5 years) are not withdrawn. Language difficulties are usually re-solved by the end of the first year in school'.
(Brittan and Townsend 1972, p.25)

These are bold statements and need a tremendous amount of serious thought, consideration and insight. One cannot generalise but I personally could not make such a categoric declaration concerning the language achievements of the immigrant and E2L children in my experience.

In the Bullock Report (referring to older children) we read:

Although after a year he [an Indian child] may seem to follow the normal curriculum, especially where oral work is concerned, the limitations to his English may be disguised . . .

Many of the mistakes are essentially those of the second language learner, such as failure to use articles in a way that comes automatically to the native speaker, or inaccurate verb forms and confused morphology.
(Department of Education and Science 1976, p.290)

With these reports in mind, a careful note was made of the ways and means in which Suba and Asad communicated during the last week of their first term, i.e. after three months in school. The following recorded observations indicate how children can disguise and overcome language inadequacies, thus giving a false impression of their genuine progress in learning to speak the English language fluently and well.

(1) Both boys had developed a code of understanding and formed a
    unique relationship with their teacher and some of the children.

Asad was playing a game with the teacher. Before they had finished he suddenly tapped her shoulder and pointed.

'Yes, in a minute,' the teacher replied. Asad's gesture was meaningless to me, but the teacher explained without any hesitation, 'He wanted to play with something else.'

When playing with the children, Asad was shop-keeper, he confidently handed fruit over the counter to his 'customers' and received their money with a smile although, apart from 'Thank you,' his speech was in Bengali.

Suba was able to tease the children in a kindly manner with a smile on his face, as he allowed only the children who were going to the toilet to pass by. Everyone accepted his 'fun' good-naturedly in spite of his limited vocabulary — 'Toilet — yes — toilet?'

(2) The boys, especially Asad, appeared to be relaxed and 'at home' in the classroom.

Asad whistled incessantly and took a great interest in everything that was going on around him. He appeared to be the only child in his class who noticed me stand up my travelling clock, and immediately came over to inspect it.

(3) The boys had learned quickly to substitute words with simple actions.

A child showed me his jersey, Asad immediately came to me, tapped my skirt and pointed to his jersey.

The teacher noticed an error in Suba's work. Without saying anything she passed him an eraser. He immediately scanned the page, saw the mistake and corrected it.

(4) Both the boys were able to reply to certain questions using different words, but not incorporating them in a sentence.

Asad was playing a game with the teacher.
    TEACHER: 'What colour are you, Asad?'
    ASAD: 'Orange.'
    TEACHER: 'What number is it, Asad?'
    ASAD: 'Two.'

The welfare helper was working with Asad.
    WELFARE HELPER: 'What colour is the van?'
    ASAD: 'Yellow.'
    WELFARE HELPER: 'How many dogs?'
    ASAD: 'One, two, three, four.'

Suba was working with clay.
    OBSERVER: What are you making — what is this, Suba?'
    SUBA: 'A dog.'

(These conversations showed a marked improvement on previous occasions when both boys had repeated the adult's questions word for word.)

(5) It appeared that the boys had learned to surmise or predict many of the teacher's remarks.

The teacher looked at the sand in the Lego box.
> TEACHER: 'Sand — who put the sand in the Lego?'
> Asad immediately pointed to Harwinder.
> TEACHER: 'Asad, take all those pieces and put them back into the box, shake the sand off, please.'
> Asad responded.

(6) There were remarks which the boys only half understood.

The teacher spoke to Suba.
> TEACHER: 'Fetch me the blue cards, please.'
> Suba went to the cards but did not know which ones were required although he easily recognised colours.

The children in Asad's class were making 'Mother's Day' cards, and they knew that they were going to take them home and give them to their mothers as a 'thank you'. It appeared that Asad did not understand what he was making or the reason for so doing, but he enjoyed the activity immensely.

(7) There were many remarks which the boys obviously did not understand.

In Asad's classroom the children sang a simple song about different parts of the body and they touched their various limbs as the names were mentioned.
Asad tried to join in, but he was always behind the other children with his actions. It was obvious that he did not understand the words and relied entirely on his ability to copy the movements of other children in order to share in the activity.

Suba had been measuring some lines which the teacher had drawn.
'Would you like to draw your own lines?' she asked.
Suba did not understand.
The teacher's efforts to explain failed and when she drew a few lines to demonstrate, Suba insisted on measuring them.

> TEACHER (to Suba): 'Draw me a picture.'
> Suba did not understand; he sat with an anxious expression on his face for five minutes.

The teacher did not know how to communicate her request because immediately she showed someone else's picture to Suba, he copied it, and she wanted him to express his own ideas on paper.

The teacher tried to adapt her demonstration and very quickly flicked through a book containing a child's drawings.

Suba noticed some people and immediately tried to copy them.

TEACHER: 'Who are these? Mummy, Daddy, Asad?'

Suba's face remained blank.

TEACHER: 'Peter, Jane?'

Suba nodded! (See p.65.)

Teacher to Suba: 'Good boy, you've tried very hard, you can go to play for a few minutes.'

Suba remained where he was, sitting on a chair.

(8) Asad's ego-centric speech was in Bengali. The boys spoke very few words in English and neither of them mastered a complete sentence. Their remarks were:

ASAD: 'Toilet.'
   'Thank you.'
SUBA: 'Look boy do.'
   'Toilet — yes — toilet?'
   'Me leader.'
   'Shut up.'
   'Come on.'

After twelve weeks attendance in school — one term — the boys showed considerable difficulty in understanding what was being said to them, particularly when the remarks had no visual indication of their meaning. The boys were not able to speak English apart from a few isolated words.

There are special difficulties, too, for very young children from non-English speaking families, children born in Britain but brought up in homes where neither the language in use nor the culture is English . . . these children, after a full two years in infant classes often reach junior school seriously lacking in fluency in English. (Department of Education and Science 1976, p.292.)

Although this case-study concerns two boys who had only recently arrived in England the findings and conclusions have a much wider significance. They can nearly all be applied to the children of overseas parentage who are born in this country but who are admitted to school unable to speak English because of their foreign culture and mother tongue. The difficulties which these children encounter (especially the first one in the family to attend school in England) are often just as real and prevalent as they were for Suba and Asad.

Advantages of a specialised language group

(1) In a one-to-one relationship or small group, an adult can discover to a certain extent an E2L child's capabilities which can then be fostered and developed. It was almost impossible for Suba's class teacher to sit quietly with him for any length of time without the interference of other children who also required her attention. It was extremely difficult for her to discover how many of the words in the matching and reading apparatus he really understood.

(2) Communicating with a child who cannot speak English is not easy. Experience and a special understanding of the child's needs and difficulties are essential if he is to receive the appropriate and relevant help required in order for him to integrate successfully and learn English as a second language. The explanations and instructions given by adults to both Suba and Asad illustrated this point on many occasions. Two simple examples were trying to explain the word 'funny' to Suba when it occurred in his reading book, and asking Asad 'to draw a picture of his family'.

(3) When the immigrant or E2L child is first admitted to school there are often different problems of custom, culture and discipline to overcome; these require the firm but understanding guidance of an adult. His sense of humour, reactions and attitudes can also differ from those of an English child. Suba and Asad had no idea of the formation of a queue when waiting for their turn on the apparatus or at dinner time — they both persisted in letting other children go in front of them! When Suba and Asad watched a play performed by a visiting theatre group, their facial expressions remained serious without a flicker of a smile although the other children were rocking with laughter.

(4) Communication with a non-English speaking child takes time. The teacher with a large class of children does not have the required time available for one child. Suba's teacher often had to cease her efforts of communication and explanation when working with him because of lack of time, and the demands which other children made upon her.

(5) Students and unqualified adults can assist the non-English speaking child in the classroom to a certain extent, but qualified experienced teachers are essential.

(6) The indigenous and other English speaking children in an infant school may pass on an English vocabulary, but they are incapable of appreciating the achievements of a non-English speaking child and cannot reinforce or encourage his efforts with the insight of an observant and experienced adult. The remarks made to Suba and Asad by their peers showed this very clearly.

(7) It is impossible for a class teacher to give the specialised help incorporating relevant materials, equipment, courses and time when she is also concentrating her energies on the needs of indigenous children and supervising a class of thirty.

(8) Communication is not always possible in spite of a child's repeated efforts to make himself understood. On these occasions he needs an adult who has both the time and the patience to give him additional reassurance. Having spent a long time working on a model, Suba was unable to tell us what he had made. (See p. 121.)

(9) Sometimes the only way of judging whether a child has understood or not, is to observe the expression on his face. If a child sits quietly he can easily be overlooked by a class teacher who has thirty other faces to watch.

(10) Even simple verbal explanations are occasionally impossible to communicate, and the child's curiosity must remain unsatisfied — thus frustrations arise which require careful handling and adult understanding. When Suba pointed to an illustration and asked what a butterfly was, it was impossible to explain.

(11) The non-English speaking child has no basic English vocabulary on which to build a more complex form of speech — it is impossible to extend his use of language in the way that an indigenous child's mother tongue is developed within the environment of the classroom. He needs careful individual help in order to learn correctly and master the English language. When I looked at a book with Suba and Asad together, Suba spent a great deal of time explaining the illustrations to Asad in Bengali. Although it was apparent that Suba had a fund of language on which to draw in connection with the contents of the book, I was unable to extend his vocabulary, and could not discern whether his concepts of certain illustrations were similar to those of an indigenous child.

It was also noticed during the observations that Asad could name a 'train', 'rabbit' and 'teddy-bear' when they were shown in one particular illustration, but he was unable to generalise and name them in different circumstances.

(12) The immigrant child has different experiences from the indigenous child and additional individual explanations are sometimes required — the class teacher either ignores the need of the immigrant child, or holds back the other children in the class while she explains something with which they are very familiar. Asad did not know what a snow-man was — he had never experienced snow.

(13) Often the only means of communication is physical and it is not always easy for a class teacher to move in order to touch or fetch a non-English speaking child (especially when there is more than one!). Many difficulties arise when a teacher cannot use words to span the distance between herself and the infants in the opposite corner of the classroom — this was particularly so in the case with Asad.

(14) The immigrant and E2L child may have to adapt to a different intonation, pitch and inflexion of voices. These can sound very confusing in a large class, especially in a multicultural school. A close relationship with one individual can help the non-English speaking child to adjust to the meanings implied by differing tones. It is difficult to discern how much a child is understanding and deliberately ignoring, but it was interesting to watch Suba smiling quietly while a West Indian child angrily reprimanded him. On another occasion the stern voice of the headmistress complaining about the untidy home corner, had an immediate effect on all the children concerned, apart from Suba, who continued to play with the tea-set unperturbed by her comments or the tone in which they were uttered!

(15) A non-English speaking child is unable to share in any past or future events through the medium of words. This excludes him from discussions following experiences such as stories, television programmes, etc., and it prevents the class teacher from preparing him for any future event.

In a large class the non-English speaking child can feel cut off from the shared experiences of the other children, especially when he can tell by their facial expressions and tone of voice that he is missing something. Individual adult help can enable him to overcome some of these difficulties providing that time is given to show the child what is going to happen whenever this is possible. Many incidents were indicative of the fact that Suba and Asad felt isolated and bewildered because of their inability to understand, particularly during group discussions.

(16) The analyses of the English words which Suba and Asad used showed that a much greater proportion were spoken to adults (see pp.64—9). This underlines the necessity for immigrant and E2L children to have plenty of opportunity to speak with adults in a one-to-one relationship.

(17) The immigrant and E2L child often lacks experience in the handling of manipulative apparatus. He requires extra help and time to experiment in this area, but he is also anxious to develop his reading and writing because:
(a) this is usually what is expected of him by his parents,
(b) this is something with which he is possibly already familiar in his own language, and
(c) if he is like Suba he is anxious not to be different from the other children.
The child placed in this situation needs a great deal of adult help in order to curtail frustration and despondency. Suba and Asad both had difficulty in handling manipulative apparatus and books.

(18) If a class is organised informally, and the children move about independently, the non-English speaking child often needs the security of the routine in a more formal withdrawal group — this was particularly noticeable with Suba.

(19) It is not always possible to foresee certain difficulties or misunderstandings which can arise even when work has been carefully planned and prepared. With English speaking children the teacher can adapt the situation accordingly through the medium of words. It is considerably more difficult to make adjustments quickly when the child cannot understand what is being said. Individual unhurried adult help is essential.
Suba's teacher spent a considerable amount of time preparing work for him, but was frequently thwarted because of the severe language difficulties and misunderstandings which arose.

(20) It is easy for a non-English speaking child who is sitting silently to be accidentally overlooked by a class teacher. This can happen

when the teacher is supervising a large number of children who are able to attract her attention with verbal requests and comments which she understands.

(21) It is easier for a teacher with a small group of children to listen for, and try to remedy, any errors which arise. Suba confused 'p' and 'f' and, although the teacher did her best to correct him, it was extremely difficult to provide the necessary help in the classroom.

(22) When a non-English speaking child is withdrawn from the classroom for a period during the day, there is no danger of the indigenous children being held back during that particular time while efforts to communicate are made. It also eases the situation where a class teacher is criticised for devoting more time and attention to the non-English speaking child than she does to the other class members.

(23) The language withdrawal group enables a child to meet with any other child or adult in the school who speaks his own language, and thus can help him to develop his own mother tongue. Suba and Asad showed a marked change when they met and conversed together during the first week.

(24) The teacher who is responsible for a small group of children is able to take them out and share different living experiences in varied situations so that the language is relevant, the vocabulary meaningful and the concepts understood and appreciated as fully as possible.

The only time I saw this happen with Suba and Asad was on one occasion when a welfare helper took Asad out to touch the playing field after he had looked at an illustration of a lamb eating grass. Because each teacher was responsible for a class of children, it was not practical for her to accompany Suba or Asad to a different situation or environment outside the immediate surroundings.

If the educational problems of immigrant children are tackled effectively while the children are still in the infant or nursery school, they are likely to present considerably less difficulty in the later school careers of these children. The problems of the junior and secondary schools will be in this respect alleviated, and the children's own prospects of benefiting from their education will be greatly extended.
(Schools Council Working Paper 13, 1967, p.10).

PART THREE
Practical recommendations

10 The class teacher

Unless one has taught children in a multicultural reception class, it is difficult to appreciate fully the pressures and problems which continually arise.

It is not always easy to form a quick relationship with a young child when you cannot ask him his name or reassure him with a word of encouragement as he ventures into school for the first time. Discipline can be extremely difficult and time-consuming when children cannot understand what is being said or have to make an extra effort to concentrate in order to grasp what they are being told. Some children play on this inability to understand, and use it as an excuse for not responding quickly.

Indigenous children become restless, bored and impatient when they are kept waiting, and if such delays are frequent the children who speak English lose the urgency of responding immediately to a teacher's request; time is wasted and the class can become disintegrated and noisy.

The level of noise is often high in a multicultural classroom because the children, and on some occasions the adults, appear to believe that they will make a person not speaking their language understand if they shout. Children who are experimenting with new sounds or trying with difficulty to express themselves may shout with effort or triumph. The intonations of different languages vary and it takes time for the immigrant and E2L children to adjust to the modulations of an English person and respond to her voice. I have noticed that some children who do not appear to understand what I am saying respond quickly to the same English statement when it is made by my Asian assistant using her native accent.

Many reception class teachers are exhausted by lunch time, let alone the end of the afternoon with their efforts to occupy and organise thirty infants, some of whom are speaking a different language. Teachers who are keen to learn and make an effort to seek advice on ways to help the immigrant and E2L children often return disheartened because so many of the skills and techniques used in teaching English as a second language can only be applied when working with a few children in a small group.

In this chapter we are going to look at some of the problems facing a class teacher and suggest ways in which a little of the stress on both adults and children might be alleviated.

Organisation – equipment and activities

One of the first pieces of advice which I pass on to students or inexperienced teachers before they embark on taking a multicultural class is to make a list of all the things which a child *can* do without understanding English, and all the things he *cannot* do, e.g.

Positive activities (can)	*Negative activities (cannot)*
Constructional toys	Discussion, news, etc.
Clay	Creative writing
Painting	Reading
Sand	Talking with indigenous children
Water	Listening to stories
Looking at illustrated books	Listening to radio and television
Copying numbers or letters	programmes
Drawing	Following suggestions, requests
Weighing and balancing	made by the teacher . . .
Home corner (which should be	
equipped with home links for the	
E2L children, e.g. sari material,	
chop sticks, etc. according to	
their nationality	
Threading beads	
Sorting and matching shapes,	
colours, pictures, etc. (Illustrations	
cut from identical sheets of	
wrapping paper are excellent for	
this purpose)	
Bricks	
Talking with children who speak	
their language . . .	

Positive activities

Having considered carefully all the activities in which a non-English speaking child is able to participate, bearing in mind cultural mismatch as well as language barriers, use them to the maximum and cut down to a minimum the situations requiring verbal explanations.

Although many immigrant and E2L children will want to select activities for themselves according to their needs, interests and abilities, it is essential for the teacher to have a definite plan in her own mind in order to establish a routine and to forestall children becoming bored, sitting silently, or interfering and perhaps hurting other children.

If possible the activities should be linked with the general organisation in the classroom so that the immigrant and E2L children are engaged in similar activities to the indigenous children and can work alongside them; a balance of interest should be maintained, i.e. constructive activities, mathematics, drawing and writing, creative work, etc.

The teacher will have to make allowances for the emotional and social needs of the non-English speaking child. If he is very withdrawn and refuses to move from a particular place, allow him to stay where he is but slowly introduce new activities by taking the equipment to him. Begin with anything which you think he can do or which links him with home (see p.140). This might mean scribbling on a piece of paper with a pencil in preference to experimenting with new crayons, however brightly coloured or attractive they may be; threading beads or even knitting can sometimes give a child the initial confidence which he needs. Allow him time to watch the other children and remember that, as long as he is made to feel secure and as relaxed as possible, he is listening and watching and silently absorbing the atmosphere even though he may appear to be doing nothing. Some children will want to experiment with everything and can become very excitable, rushing from one occupation to another, upsetting the equipment and disturbing other children. These children need a very definite routine, and the teacher may have to restrict their activities at first. Ensure that they are given interesting but clear-cut occupations into which they can channel their energy and enthusiasm, and also reach and achieve success and satisfaction.

Having planned an initial programme of activities it is important for the teacher to find ways of extending each experience. A child may not be able to speak English but he may be highly intelligent and easily become bored. Assignment cards without using words are invaluable and they can be kept for further use. If a teacher spends a little time pondering over even one piece of equipment, e.g. a box of animals for sorting, it is surprising how many different assignments involving matching, colour, shape, counting, drawing, writing, etc. can be developed and cards made accordingly.

Clay, junk modelling, paint and other messy or group activities are creative areas and although feasible the teacher needs to be aware of the difficulties which they may present.

(1) Many minority-group children will not have met these materials before and find the initial feel of them repugnant. They may need to watch other children using them before gaining the necessary confidence and desire to experiment for themselves.
(2) Some children will want to dabble or experiment wholeheartedly with the materials, but will not know how to set about it – they have to be shown what the paste is for or how to hold a brush.
(3) Many minority-group children do not like getting their clothes dirty, and suitable aprons must be readily available where the child can reach one for himself – he should also be shown how to fasten and unfasten it.
(4) These particular activities require the children to think for themselves rather than being told exactly what to do – this is sometimes very difficult in the early stages when the children do not understand what is expected of them.
(5) Group activities such as the sand or home corner frequently give rise to verbal communication between English and non-English speaking children – the latter are placed at a disadvantage which may frustrate them.
(6) Handling and piecing together constructional toys or puzzles may prove to be strange and confusing to the minority group child who has no previous experience of similar equipment. Do not push him into these activities, but ensure that he has the opportunity to select them if he so wishes. Adult assistance is sometimes necessary at first, and time should also be allowed for the child to watch others using the equipment until he finally shares in the activity of his own accord.

It is important for the E2L child to be given a measure of responsibility from the very beginning. He should have somewhere to keep his personal belongings and know exactly where it is and what it is for. Insist that he co-operates in the general organisation of the classroom, i.e. putting equipment away, sweeping up the sand if he has been using

As Suba watched the children pursuing their varied activities, he frequently appeared to be lost and wandered aimlessly around until the teacher sat beside him and gave him a specific task to do.

Introducing the English language

As we have already indicated, it is impossible to expect a class teacher to be entirely responsible for teaching English as a second language. The majority of concentrated work should be undertaken by a specialist teacher working with a group. However, many class teachers are left to carry out this work alone, so let us see what can be done under such circumstances.

The teacher needs to have a clear understanding of the underlying principles laid down in the earlier chapters of this book; she should then apply them to her own situation and ask the following questions:

Are the young E2L children relaxed and being given a sense of security so that their ego-centric speech is used and developed naturally?

Are the children being given opportunities to converse in their own language?

Are the children being pressurised into group activities with which they really cannot cope, or are they happily occupied and able to listen to the conversation around them undisturbed?

Has the teacher read appropriate books on learning English as a second language which include information concerning language structure and patterns? (This should assist her in knowing how to converse with the child whilst he is playing or showing her his work.) (Derrick 1966; Garvie 1976; City of Bradford Metropolitan Council 1978.)

Has the teacher planned and prepared certain activities from which a particular vocabulary will develop, e.g. dressing-up clothes; a bag of objects; specific utensils or provisions in the home corner; pictures on the wall; making books on one subject, i.e. 'Myself', 'My family', 'My house', etc.?

Very often we categorise and 'pigeon hole' language teaching, but we must remember it goes on all the time. Whatever we are doing and wherever we are, language can be introduced — when the children are having their milk, washing their hands, doing up their coats and shoes, always there are opportunities for teaching language, but the adult must be aware of how she is phrasing her speech and, if possible, have some pattern and purpose in the vocabulary she uses during a particular time.

During my observations of Suba I watched a student supervising certain periods.

Day 37. Week 9

The children were making paper hats and decorating them with individual designs. Suba had completed his pattern, working silently, unlike the other children who discussed their efforts with each other.

Suba had been in the classroom for forty minutes and the only words which had been spoken to him were 'get off' by a child who had pushed him from his chair — Suba had retaliated with 'ger-off'.

He lifted his paper hat from the table and carried it to the student who was busily stapling those belonging to other children; she did not notice Suba and walked away.

Suba followed.

A child put on his hat — Suba smiled.

The student turned, she picked up Suba's hat and stapled it then placed it on Suba's head — but she did not speak a word to him.

How easy it is for us to miss a valuable opportunity.

The two analyses of the adults' remarks to Suba and Asad emphasised the difference in the phraseology and reinforcement of speech used by the reception class teacher. Her language, adapted for five-year-old children, was more suited to the needs of the E2L child than the speech used by the teacher responsible for the seven-year-olds.

The case-study also emphasised the use which a teacher can make of other children in the older classes, i.e. the older children are more capable of showing or trying to explain something to a non-English speaking child. Consideration, however, must be given to the limitations of even the oldest children in the infant school, particularly when they act as interpreters for a teacher. In an infant school six- and seven-year-old children have to be relied upon as interpreters, and, as we have seen, their experience and concepts of language are naturally more limited than those of older children (see p.30).

Routine in language. Not only is routine important within the organisation and planning of the classroom activities for the non-English speaking child, it is also essential that the teacher has a form of routine in the language which she uses day by day.

The reception class teacher was more definite and deliberate with her remarks to the children (see number of commands, p.83) and she used similar phrases alongside the regular routine of activities; for example:

'Everybody come and sit down. Come and sit down on the floor. Come and sit by me. That's right, come along. Now the Green group go and fetch a pencil, then sit in the writing corner. That's right, good, yes, go and fetch a pencil, then sit in the writing corner and I will bring you your books . . . '

Because of the age group of the children the routine was more rigid and the language more explicit and repetitive.

It is important for all teachers of E2L children to ensure that the same phrases are repeated regularly and not too many variations used within a short space of time: for example, avoid 'Please close the door', 'Can you shut the door?' 'Push the door to, it's so draughty', or 'It's time to go out to play', 'We'll stop now for break', 'Goodness it's playtime – we'd better finish there'.

In Suba's class valuable stimulation for conversation and written or creative work was provided in the form of questions such as 'What do you think . . . ?', 'Would you like to . . . ?', 'Why was he . . . ?' Many activities allowed the children to make personal choices after the teacher had inspired their interest with carefully chosen leading questions.

Some of the seven-year-olds were not yet capable of easily acquiring the information which they sought from books, and a great deal of their learning involved questions: 'Why does it do that?', 'What is this for?', 'When are we going . . . ?' etc. Frequently the teacher would encourage the children to think for themselves before giving them a direct answer, e.g. 'Well, what do you think?' This form of conversation which is so right for the English speaking seven-year-olds is meaningless and confusing to a non-English speaking child of the same age, whose mind is probably abounding with the same questions, and who longs to take part in the eager discussion around him – a situation such as this can be desperately frustrating.

Introducing reading material

Parents of new arrivals into Britain have, on several occasions, assured me that although their children cannot speak English they can read it! On investigation I have found that they have memorised, in some cases, the first three books of a reading scheme, and can select words on request without any idea as to what they mean.

This pseudo-reading may appear obvious in the early stages, but unless it is checked it can present serious undetected problems later on. Older children who have developed the habit of reading without comprehension find that apart from their failure to enjoy books, they cannot easily refer to them for information and become hopelessly confused in their efforts to study at a later stage. How many E2L children are in remedial groups in the secondary schools for this very reason?

When selecting reading books for E2L children, I consider the content before the vocabulary, although both must of course be carefully analysed because the obvious reasons for choice may not necessarily be the best.

For instance we recently purchased two reading schemes in my school. One was chosen particularly for the E2L children because it included people of different nationalities and the books were very short with simple repetitive phraseology. The other scheme was selected with the indigenous children in mind because it was related to their experiences in an English home background. After using the books for a short length of time we realised that the content of the latter scheme was in actual fact more suitable for, and preferred by, our non-English speaking children. Why? Because the introductory words in the second scheme involved actions, e.g. 'I can jump, I can ride', and the words at the beginning of the first scheme introduced characters. It is considerably easier to explain an action to a non-English speaking child because he can experience it, often in varying circumstances, and relate it to himself — in this particular instance 'I can jump high, I can jump over the bricks, I can jump down the steps, I can jump on to the mat, I can jump into the hole, I can ride on the bicycle, I can ride in the car, we can ride in the bus' etc.

The concept of a fictitious character was a little more difficult to explain; it was something in which the child was unable to participate actively and was remote from his own personal surroundings and activities even when the illustrations and names bore a resemblance to his own culture.

I shall not attempt to enlarge upon the skills of teaching reading apart from mentioning the following:

(1) I do believe that there is a place for an E2L child in the older age group of an infant school to meet and experiment with word symbols, pre-reading material and even a reading book if he so

desires whilst he is learning the English language — providing the
material is closely linked with his language work and experience.
(2) It is imperative that a teacher does not accept the child's memor-
ising of symbols as reading. She must ensure that he understands
the concepts behind the printed page before he is given a more
difficult and complicated book (see pp.149—50). The child should
ideally understand the spoken words before he is presented with
their written symbols in the early stages.
(3) The vocabulary should be simple and the phraseology short and
repetitive. New words and different tenses should be introduced
with care and repetition both in the reading material and with the
teacher during language activities.
(4) The teacher should make a detailed analysis of the reading material
before the child uses it so that she knows exactly what he is trying
to learn and its relevance to the English vocabulary which he is
developing during the general school activities.

The reading material used in infant schools should be truthful and unsentimental
in its visual and verbal content.
(Department of Education and Science 1976, p.286.)

Problems of time and tenses

Time

Anyone who has had the experience of trying to hold a conversation
with a person who cannot understand his language realises the length
of time it takes to communicate even a simple comment; and yet
little allowance is made for this aspect which is apparently overlooked
in many multicultural schools where the non-English speaking children
are left to integrate and learn without any additional help from adults.

The content of the remarks made by the teachers to Suba and Asad
clearly emphasise the extra time which is needed in order to explain
a simple task to a non-English speaking child.

The following example shows how Suba's teacher took half an hour
to explain to Suba that she wanted him to stick the correct number
of stars beside the figures written in his book. The teacher had carefully prepared the page remembering that Suba could count from one
to twenty in English, knowing that it was an activity well within his
capability and incorporating his eagerness to use his book. She hoped

that it would prove a simple and satisfying activity which he would enjoy because he had a fascination for a packet of gummed coloured stars which he had found in her desk.

Day 4. Week 1. 1.25 p.m.
It was Suba's turn to work in the mathematics area. The teacher was supervising him in a group of six children and she had drawn some circles in his book with a figure underneath each one. (On the previous day Suba had enjoyed writing '1', '2', '3', '4', '5', and colouring in the correct number of objects for each amount.)

The teacher pointed to the circle with a 4.

SUBA: 'Four.'

The teacher pointed to a packet of stars on the table and then pointed to the circle.

Suba stuck on one star by the figure 4.

TEACHER: 'One, two, three, four.'

The teacher pointed to the picture on the wall and counted four objects adjacent to the figure 4.

TEACHER: 'One, two, three, four.'

The teacher stuck on three more by Suba's one.

TEACHER: 'One, two, three, four.'

Suba looked at the other figures which the teacher had written on the page. He stuck one star beneath each figure regardless of the amount symbolised.

The teacher pointed to the figure 5.

SUBA: 'Five.'

The teacher moved some unifix cubes towards him and pointed to them — she started to count them.

TEACHER: 'One . . . '

SUBA: 'Two, three, four, five.'

[When Suba counted the cubes, his one-to-one relationship was satisfactory — he just did not appear to understand that the teacher wanted him to stick five stars in the circle beside the figure 5, etc.]

The teacher pointed to the stars and then to the 5. 'More, more, Suba.'

Suba looked at the page and then at the teacher, there was no other response.

TEACHER: 'Five, Suba, five.'

The teacher finally pushed four stars over to Suba, then, pointing to the five, she had to leave him to supervise the other children.

Suba picked the stars up one by one, licked them carefully and stuck them on beside the one already there.

The teacher returned, she slowly counted the stars pointing to each one in turn, 'One, two, three, four, five.' She drew another circle and wrote '5' beneath it.

TEACHER: 'Suba, five.' She pointed to the 5 and then to the stars, pulling five away from the pile.

TEACHER: 'Five.'

She then pointed to the circle.

TEACHER: 'Five.'

She pointed to five empty places in the circle.

Suba understood — he steadily stuck on five. The teacher drew another circle and wrote '5'.

Suba immediately without any hesitation pulled out five stars and stuck them on correctly.

1.55 p.m.

Suba repeated the exercise using 3 and 6 successfully.

It might be thought that Suba should have been left to sort or experiment with equipment which did not require any explanation during the first week, but sorting apparatus appeared to be unfamiliar to him and he persisted in fetching his book and pencil and sitting with children who were working with mathematics cards. Once he had understood the instructions he worked with ease and pleasure.

In a busy classroom it is sometimes impossible for a teacher to find the time to explain an activity to a child, and she is forced to leave him, hoping that he will discover what to do, perhaps by watching other children or using his own past experience or 'common sense'. In many cases these fail.

Day 3. Week 1. 10.50 a.m.

[The class was supervised by an additional part-time teacher.]

TEACHER: 'Suba, you are going to write in your book. Over there, Suba.'

The teacher pointed to the 'writing table' in the corner of the room and Suba walked over to it. His writing book had been placed ready for him and he opened it and found his drawing from a previous day. Five other children joined him and the teacher went to supervise them. Each child was given some letters. The children began to write words connected with their specific letters, and they drew pictures to illustrate them. The teacher was very busy supervising other children — Suba sat and watched.

11.10 a.m.

Suba drew a circle attached to a stick on the same page as yesterday's drawing.

11.25 a.m.

The teacher called over to Suba.

TEACHER: 'Are you doing a nice picture for me?'

Suba turned the page over.

11.30 a.m.

Suba turned to another page and started to crayon. The teacher moved towards him and looked at his picture.

'That's lovely, Suba, good boy.'

[Suba had sat for forty minutes before he attempted to crayon a picture. When he drew the circle attached to a stick, he seemed uncertain as to what was expected of him.]

Tenses

An additional problem, which faces every teacher who is trying to explain an activity to a child who cannot understand English, is the inability to communicate information concerning the past or the future.

It is comparatively easy to convey to a child that you want him to draw a picture, but to explain that you want him to illustrate something which he has seen or experienced in the past, or to draw a picture of a possible future incident, is quite another matter. He may copy another child's impression, but to explain to him that you want his own individual ideas is virtually impossible (see pp.96–7).

A considerable amount of the conversation between a teacher and seven-year-old children is connected with past or future events such as a discussion after a story or a television programme, or shared accounts of personal experiences.

An example of this problem occurred in the observations of Suba.

Day 8. Week 2. 11.30 a.m.
Suba returned to the classroom having watched a television programme with his class; the other children were holding a general discussion about the dinosaurs which they had seen. Suba entered the room alone. Some children asked the teacher if they could write stories and paint pictures about the weird and wonderful creatures so fresh and alive in their memories and imaginations, and the teacher encouraged their ideas and suggestions. The children took out their books and everyone soon appeared to be busily engaged in various activities, many connected with dinosaurs.

11.40 a.m.
Suba sat down. He pulled his writing book out from a pile on the table and opened it at random. He crayoned an orange 'sky' and brown 'ground'.
    TEACHER: 'Can you draw what you have seen, Suba? Television, Suba. Draw a
             dinosaur – television.'
    The teacher pointed to his book and then to the other children's illustrations of half-completed dinosaurs drawn in a varied assortment of shapes, colours and sizes.
    TEACHER: 'Dinosaur, television, Suba.' The children helpfully pointed to
their works of art.
    CHILD: 'Suba – dinosaurs, draw a dinosaur, Suba. Draw what you saw on the
           television, Suba. Draw one like this.'
    Suba showed no response, he sat quite still.

11.50 a.m.
Suba continued to sit watching the other children drawing. He held a pencil in his hand turning it round between his thumb and fingers.

The other children worked busily on, a buzz of conversation indicated the questions and comments, the wonder and interest which filled their minds as they pondered on these great beasts of long ago. The teacher encouraged their efforts. 'Good, good, that's lovely — well done!'

11.55 a.m.
Suba continued to sit.

The teacher turned to a group of Asian children.

'Please could you try to explain to Suba what to do in your language?'

[Although Suba did not speak Punjabi the teacher hoped that one or two words might prove meaningful and penetrate the barrier between her and her non-English pupil.]

The two Indian girls waved their hands and dramatically flourished their own drawings as they delivered a string of fluent Punjabi which came to a triumphant end with 'OK?' [This conversation was recorded on tape and was a very good exposition on how a dinosaur should be drawn, but the Punjabi language bore no similarity to Suba's Bangladesh dialect of Bengali. How important it is for teachers not to presume that all Asian children, or children from another continent, can automatically understand one another or have a common element in their languages and dialects — this is not necessarily so.]

The teacher looked at Narinder. 'Did Suba understand?' Narinder reassured her. 'I think he understands, but he doesn't know how to do it.'

Rita, the second interpreter, had an idea. 'I'll do it for you,' she announced emphatically. Taking Suba's pencil she turned to a clean page in his book and began to draw.

Suba tried to push her hand away but Rita persisted.

Suba picked up a crayon to colour the creature, but immediately both the Indian girls grabbed the crayons and vigorously coated the dinosaur in green — they pushed Suba's hand away.

NARINDER: 'Wait, wait.'

The two girls made Suba wait until they had completely crayoned the dinosaur. Suba watched.

The children added the final finishing touches and then walked away.

Suba looked at the drawing, half-heartedly he added some spikes to the lower part of the creature's abdomen, and then turned to the clean adjoining page. Painstakingly he began to draw a replica of the dinosaur to the best of his ability.

The children left for dinner; the classroom was empty all except for Suba who, undeterred by the silence, remained alone until he had completed his own, personal dinosaur! 12.20 p.m.

Asad suffered in a slightly different way from this lack of communication concerning past or future events. When the children in his class were preparing for their first PE lesson in the hall, the teacher took great pains to explain to them exactly what was going to happen and why it was important to remove some of their clothing. Not only was the teacher able to reassure them about this future event, but the children were able to express and communicate to her their own personal anxieties.

Day 3. Week 1.

1ST CHILD: 'I don't want to take my clothes off.'

TEACHER: 'That's all right, if you don't want to you needn't.'

2ND CHILD: 'I don't want to go on the apparatus.'

TEACHER: 'That's all right, you can watch.'

3RD CHILD: 'I only want to take off my jumper.'

TEACHER: 'All right, I don't mind, perhaps you will take off your shirt next time.'

4TH CHILD: 'Where are you going?'

TEACHER: 'In the hall, you know, the big hall down the stairs.'

5TH CHILD: 'I don't want to take off my clothes.'

TEACHER: 'That's all right, don't cry, my dear.'

6TH CHILD: 'Do I have to take off my shoes?'

TEACHER: 'No, leave your shoes on to walk to the hall.'

Asad watched. There was no reason as far as he was concerned for the children to be undressing. A student tried to remove his pullover. He shook his head indicating 'No'.

The teacher tried to reassure him: 'All right, Asad, don't worry.' These words were meaningless to the child who at that moment had no idea as to why someone was suddenly trying to undress him. The routine had changed and Asad's security had momentarily crumbled – all he could do was to watch and wait.

Even when a non-English speaking child has made a tremendous effort to comply with the expectations and activities in the classroom, it is sometimes impossible to appreciate what is in his mind and what he has really achieved.

In the reception class it is not always easy to recognise children's pieces of creative work, nor is it always wise to ask, but in the older age group of an infant school the children are usually anxious to tell you what they have made and why, explaining minute details as to how their creation works or what it does. In my own school children are encouraged to write about their models, and their work is often extended into areas of reading and mathematics.

When a child is unable even to tell you what he has made, there is no basis on which to build, indeed no starting point from which to begin any form of language work whether it be spoken or written. The child too must miss the tremendous sense of satisfaction which the other children gain through discussing their work with the teacher and being commended for their efforts.

Day 31. Week 7.
The teacher held up Suba's cardboard model.

TEACHER: 'Suba, what is it? Is it a lighthouse or a deep sea diver? What is
it? Is it this?'

She pointed to a large painting of a child's impression of a lighthouse.

There was no response from Suba.

ENGLISH CHILD: 'I don't think it's a lighthouse because it hasn't got a
front.'

TEACHER: 'Well, perhaps he hasn't finished it.'

(Everyone led into the hall for Assembly.)

The children returned and the teacher told them to hurry and get on with
their work.

Suba stood, his hands clasped — he yawned.

He looked at the children playing with the sand. He yawned again.

TEACHER: 'Suba.' She held up his model, 'Are you going to finish painting
this?'

Suba smiled and reached out for his work — he stood it on the shop counter
and walked away.

TEACHER: 'Are you going to finish it, Suba?

Bring me the box.

The box, Suba. [She pointed to the junk box.]

The box.

Yes, Suba, bring me the box.'

Suba touched the box.

TEACHER: 'Yes, good boy, bring it.'

She pulled cartons out of the junk box.

TEACHER: 'Come on, turn out all this stuff, love.

Come on, have a look and see what there is.

Come on, Suba, here look.'

The teacher left Suba. He worked hard, cutting and sticking pieces carefully
together with his agile fingers. The children around him chatted to each other,
but he remained silent, concentrating only on his own intricate creation. Thirty
minutes passed.

The headmistress came into the classroom and watched him.

ENGLISH CHILD TO HEADMISTRESS: 'Suba's made a model.'

HEADMISTRESS: 'What is it?'

ENGLISH CHILD: 'It looks like an umbrella.'

HEADMISTRESS: 'Go and see if you can find out.'

ENGLISH CHILD TO SUBA: 'What is it?'

Suba continued to work silently on his model for one hour, then lifting it
up he took it over to a helper.

HELPER: 'Suba, that *is* lovely. Is that grass, or is it a bed?'

Suba walked away, he held it proudly in front of the teacher.

TEACHER: 'Good boy, good boy, what is it?'

Suba went and washed his hands . . . [We never knew!]

The problems associated with 'time' and 'tense' are among the most frustrating ones to try and solve in the classroom; indeed, it is imposs-ible to find a really satisfactory solution to any degree, and both the non-English and the English speaking children can suffer as a result.

Regular routine helps to a certain extent, but the most satisfactory answer is either to provide additional adult help in the classroom, or to withdraw the non-English speaking children to a small group for part of the day, where there is time to experience as well as to explain.

When a class teacher is faced with such problems and realises the serious need for additional help, she should try to be explicit concern-ing the particular difficulties confronting her and not simply express a general sense of failure or inadequacy on either her part or that of the child. Making a quick note of difficulties as they arise and the time spent in dealing with them is valuable. Discussing and thinking them through afterwards with the other members of staff can ease the strain and tension which so easily builds up in a teacher trying to cope alone with a hard and complex situation in her classroom; it should also make her and others realise that she is probably not the only one facing such difficulties. The head teacher can also use detailed relevant information to strengthen his request for additional staff, and offer suggestions for help.

Highlighting definite problems and bringing them into the open is, to my mind, far better than keeping them suppressed and fester-ing — an attitude which easily undermines the essential happy atmos-phere of a school.

Developing the mother tongue

We have seen in chapter 5 that the development of the mother tongue is an important issue which should be given a great deal of careful consideration.

I am not suggesting for one moment that the class teacher, who has so many demands on her time, energy and skills, should be expected to develop a variety of unknown languages as well as cope with the complexities of teaching a group of thirty or more infant children from assorted backgrounds and nationalities. I do consider, however, that it is important for her to be aware of the need for each child to be encouraged in the use of his mother tongue during part of the school day.

Parents can be invited to come into school and to participate in

group work or the school assembly using their own language, even if
it is only for a few minutes. The transformation which takes place on
the faces of the Asian children when suddenly they hear their own
mother tongue in the hall never ceases to move me and impress upon
me the vital necessity of making regular opportunities for such communication. Grandmothers and mothers have brought saris into our
school to show to the children, and older sisters have supervised cooking groups teaching us how to make chapatis and other sweetmeats.
Parents of all nationalities have joined groups of children for tea and
'school made' cakes.

Indian girls from the senior school have visited us on a regular
weekly basis in order to tell a story to the Punjabi speaking children
in their own language. The girls always leave with a new book from
which to prepare the next week's story. Visits such as these play a
very important part in the education of the Indian children and are
an essential contribution towards the language development in our
school for the following reasons:

(1) The sheer enjoyment of adults and children sharing the Punjabi
    language together in school.
(2) The enrichment of the children's natural language development
    in their mother tongue (as opposed to the more artificial and
    restricted development connected with the learning of a second
    language).
(3) The Indian children are given an opportunity to participate with
    ease, enabling them to discuss, question and comment freely.
(4) Hearing the stories in their own mother tongue helps the children
    to realise that literature is not limited to a single language, but it
    is communicated through languages including their own.
(5) The Indian children are able to build up their own basic fund of
    well-known stories as soon as they enter school, without having
    to wait until they can understand English. The strain of sitting
    still and listening to a voice which conveys only a distorted
    version of the tale, or perhaps nothing at all, can ruin a child's
    early joy of sharing a heritage of literature which belongs to us
    all — a heritage which was originally collated from many countries
    and frequently had to be translated into English before the
    different generations in our land could understand, enjoy and
    pass on the stories which we now take so much for granted as
    part of our tradition.

Our local librarian has also supplied us with a selection of children's books written in Hindustani, Punjabi and Urdu. Apart from using these books in school, they are borrowed by the Asian mothers who are literate in these languages, and the stories are read to the children in their own homes.

The senior girls discuss different aspects of school life with the children, asking them about the creative activities and work displayed in the room. Reference is made to other books — occasionally the books used specifically for the teaching of reading, ensuring that the children understand the content before the teacher tries to explain it. at a later stage, in English (see pp.149—50).

It is important for these girls to have their groups of children either in the classroom or in the language room (even if the only convenient time is during the lunch hour) and not in a corridor or cloakroom, so that easy reference can be made to the children's daily activities.

During the past few years we have been fortunate enough to have an Indian assistant who speaks and writes all the languages of the Asian families represented in our school. She has continued the work of the older girls and has the Asian children every day for conversation and stories in their own mother tongue. If a six- or seven-year-old child from India or Pakistan is admitted, the assistant will spend time explaining the various activities to him, particularly those connected with mathematics which often mean something to the newcomer and enable him to show a certain degree of skill and ability. The child is immediately given a sense of security, and he converses freely in his own language until he has mastered sufficient English to cope with the school and his requirements. Because the pressure of solely confining his communication to English is released, he is, I believe, more relaxed and more able and willing to experiment with the new language — and, of course, the strange surroundings.

Having a member of staff who can speak the mother tongue of our Asian children has played an invaluable part in the enrichment and extension of the children's vocabularies. They no longer miss the opportunity and joy of hearing, discovering and using new aesthetic words because so often the experiences they share with indigenous children are discussed in two languages. For example, the nursery teacher brought a baby rabbit into school one morning. As she showed it to the Asian children, she had to use simple basic language in order for them to understand — 'Look at his ears. Can you see his eyes? Look at his tail' etc. But then the Asian assistant showed it to the same children and in their language she said: 'Look at his ears, aren't they long and pointed! Can you see how his eyes shine, what colour are they?—Watch his inquisitive little nose, it's twitching isn't it! Feel how soft and fluffy his tail is. You stroke him gently — he will not hurt you, can you feel how silky his fur is? Would you like to hold him?' What a difference, and how essential it is for all children to have this enrichment of language throughout these early years. Once they have had the knowledge and understanding of aesthetic words and the opportunity to use them in their mother tongue, the children's speech and creative writing will continue to develop until they are able to express themselves in English. Could some of the difficulties which E2L children have in writing essays at a later stage stem from the fact that during the time they were in the infant school, when the foundations for good creative writing should have been laid, the children were working in a vacuum caught between two languages, their thoughts hemmed in by the redundancy of their mother tongue and the stilted limitations of a new English vocabulary, with only a bare minimum of stimulation and enrichment from conversation, stories and poetry?

One further complication which may arise in the infant school is the difficulty concerning a child who is learning to read and write his own language at home or in evening classes.

During the latter part of the nineteen-fifties there was a considerable amount of controversy between the teachers whom I met in Haringey when the Greek and Turkish Cypriots in that area started their own language classes. It is true that these groups were held during the evenings on the school premises, several in our particular building, and the children concerned would return to school on the following morning tired and unrefreshed, but much of the criticism stemmed from the fact that this additional form of studying was undermining the work being carried out by the English teachers during the day.

At present some children in my school are studying Arabic for an hour each morning before breakfast and so the problem continues.

Every teacher working in a cosmopolitan area should be prepared to face and accept this problem by looking at the 'wholeness' of the situation. If we were in another country would we want our own children to learn to read English? Are we educating the children solely for the English education system or for the wider expectations of life which would involve their own culture or country? Do we inflict standards and pressures on ourselves, and the children, by aiming to send all of them 'up to the junior school' with the ability to read and write regardless of specific language difficulties (pseudo-reading frequently develops in these cases)?

We should never try to ignore the fact that a child is studying in another language outside school hours, because the additional work can seriously affect both his health and his progress in school; nor should we discourage or condemn such efforts without giving serious consideration to the following three points:

(1) When is the child having lessons? Is he suffering physically, i.e. having insufficient sleep or relaxation?
(2) How do the sub-skills of reading and writing his language vary from the sub-skills of reading and writing English?
(3) In what ways are these sub-skills similar in both languages?

(1) The question of time and tiredness is important and should be discussed by the parents and teachers together. A compromise should be made if possible according to the circumstances. (a) The time of the lesson should be reasonable and enable the child to have sufficient sleep. (b) The length of the lesson should be limited so that the child is able to relax between his school activities and his tuition and his bedtime. If necessary the possibility of children receiving tuition in their own language in school should be considered — this aspect is being developed in the Bedfordshire EEC project.

(2) and (3) The child should be encouraged to bring his work into school. (a) The other children and the adults can acknowledge his achievements in this field. (b) The teacher should endeavour to see both the variations and similarities in the skills involved.

I have found that it helps a child to associate the one set of skills with a particular situation, i.e. letter formation and pre-reading activities (such as left-to-right eye movements) should be introduced and practised methodically in the environment of an English classroom. The skills connected with the immigrant or E2L child's own language should be practised outside the school or, if possible, in another room.

It is to be expected that the child will be confused during the early stages of reading and writing in two languages, but, given time, he will adjust and cope with the variations of movement, symbols and sounds. He will possibly make slower progress than a child learning the skills in one language only, and he may not be able to achieve the same standard as the indigenous children in the early part of the junior or even middle school.

Referring to MacNamara's study and survey of available research concerning Irish children, Wilkinson writes:

MacNamara (1966) finds evidence that the linguistic and educational attainments of bilinguals are inferior to those of monoglots, they develop less well in both languages . . . It seems clear that learning a second language imposes a burden on development in both languages and on educational attainment. If, on the other hand it is felt desirable to learn another language, then, on the whole the earlier this can begin the better, the problems involved being taken into account and compensated for.
(Wilkinson 1971, p.99.)

There is, however, other evidence to the contrary, and when we consider the progress made by many bilingual Welsh and Swiss children, we realise what a debatable issue this is, one that warrants much serious time, thought and research — it is a subject far beyond the scope of this book.

It must be emphasised that although it is important for an immigrant and E2L child to be given the opportunity to speak, read and write in his own language, other areas of learning, such as mathematics, should incorporate the methods used within the school even if they are taught in both languages, and a concerted effort made by both parents and teachers not to confuse the child unnecessarily.

Physical contact between adults and children

Physical contact is essential in the multicultural infant classroom. Not only can it replace words and indicate to a certain degree what a child or adult is trying to say, it can also give much needed comfort and reassurance, and play an important part in overcoming the many invisible barriers which exist between strangers of all ages, races, cultures, creeds and colours. Never be afraid of physical contact with the children in the infant school. The English race is often considered to be reserved and undemonstrative, but a child's awareness of his being loved and cared for is the most important ingredient needed to make him feel welcome when he cannot speak the language. This does not mean that non-English speaking children should be smothered with caresses and constantly cuddled and petted; well meaning helpers, students or older children are sometimes inclined to do this especially if the child is small and attractive, or perhaps the only dark skinned member of the class.

Opportunities continually arise for making unostentatious physical contacts with young children, particularly in the reception groups. During the general activities of the day the understanding teacher will reach out physically towards a child, especially one with whom she cannot speak, in as many ways as possible.

In the study of Suba and Asad an analysis was made of the number of physical contacts made between each boy and adults within the school, i.e. teachers, welfare helpers and students (see pp.85—6). The figures emphasised the comparison between the number of physical contacts which adults are likely to make towards a five-year-old and a child aged seven. It is natural to hold a five-year-old's hand as you walk along together, or assist him in fastening his coat or tying his shoe laces; it is equally natural to leave an older child to wander on his own or walk beside you without any physical contact, and it is right to encourage him to be independent and expect him to do things for himself. These figures obviously reflect the personalities of both the teachers and children involved, but they do also reflect the opportunities which are certain to arise in any reception class, and the advantage which a five-year-old child has over the seven-year-old child in this particular aspect.

Social contacts

Physical contacts between two people of different colour, even when one is a child, can have very important social implications. I well remember one of the English parents in my school objecting to the Indian assistant holding her child's hand and taking her to the toilet. An English teacher must not forget that the children with dark skins in her class may never before have been touched by a 'white' person, they may even have been forbidden to have contact with such an adult. It is important for the teacher to show that there is nothing to be afraid of, and nothing wrong or distasteful about touching someone whose complexion is of a different shade or colour. The reader may consider that such a comment is entirely uncalled for and unnecessary in an infant school, but sometimes incredible barriers of prejudice lie hidden within the thoughts of adults, and these in turn are passed on to the children.

An English mother spoke to me a short while ago: 'I just could not accept these coloured people, I can't explain it, I hated to see them in the school or even in the street, and I couldn't bear to touch them. I told my child that she could have any friends she wanted home to tea as long as they weren't coloured. Then one day she asked if Rita could come home to play. Unsuspectingly I said "Yes", and Rita turned out to be "coloured". Well, I couldn't send her away, she had to come in, and do you know, she was sweet. She often comes now and all my feeling against the colour has gone — she's just like any other child, and even nicer than some.'

There are occasionally cultural reasons for avoiding certain physical contacts and these must be acknowledged with sensitivity. I have known girls who, for religious and cultural reasons, are forbidden to hold hands with boys, even in the infant school. An extension of this custom can be seen in the way in which men and women sometimes greet each other. I noticed on several occasions that a charming Asian father appeared to be very reluctant to shake hands with me. I then watched him greet my Asian assistant — instead of shaking hands they placed their own hands together and nodded to each other. Afterwards when I spoke to her about this matter, my assistant explained that in their country an adult male and female never touch each other's hands unless they are married.

Disciplinary contacts

There is of course another aspect of physical contact between the child and adult within the classroom which must be briefly referred to — the disciplinary contact.

One of the most frustrating situations which arises in the classroom is when a child who does not understand English is disruptive or excessively disobedient and the teacher is unable to reason or reprimand verbally. I must confess that I still become exasperated when trying to unravel behaviour difficulties involving non-English speaking children.

Two children enter my room, one is crying and shouting at the other in a language which I do not understand, and it is impossible to ask what has happened or find the cause of distress — 'He did it' is often the only intelligible phrase! In the classroom a piece of equipment may be missing, a child may deliberately damage another child's piece of work or construction, and these incidents are not infrequent

when the children themselves are frustrated because of their inability
to communicate. How does one deal with such situations when words
are virtually of no avail?

There is no straightforward solution, but there is a danger. In such
circumstances as these it is very easy for a teacher to resort to quick
corporal punishment, especially if she knows that the parents themselves smack or possibly beat the child and will support her actions.
These occasions are ones which place undue strain on the teacher,
but, however frustrated she is, I do advise her to refrain from smack-
ing a child.

All children understand 'No', and are aware when they have dis-
pleased the teacher. Any circumstances which may lead to the trouble
re-occurring should be avoided, for example by separating two children
for a while. The teacher should question herself as to why the child
might have resorted to disagreeable behaviour in the first place. Was
it because of circumstances in the school, e.g. was he bored? Was he
frustrated because he could not achieve something? Was he in a group
activity and, not being able to make himself understood, snatched a
piece of equipment from another child? Or was it because of home
circumstances? Was he tired due to overcrowded sleeping accommodation? Were his parents working in different shifts causing a degree
of insecurity in his life? Had he any toys at home or was a lack of
play equipment there, tempting him to take school apparatus away
with him? What time was he arriving at school in the morning —
possibly very early involving a long wait in a damp cold atmosphere
and perhaps without having had any breakfast? There are many reasons
for a child becoming fretful and unco-operative which may not stem
from inadequate language.

If a child is continually causing trouble it is advisable to seek the
help of an understanding, reliable adult who speaks the language and
is qualified to act as interpreter. The child's parent may or may not
be invited at this stage; it depends on the circumstances. If possible
I prefer to reason with the child alone through an interpreter before
the parents become involved, but this can only take place when a
member of the school staff is bilingual — it would be wrong to con-
sult an outsider about a child's difficulties before informing the
parents.

Working through behaviour difficulties with children who cannot
speak English requires much time and endless patience, and it is an

aspect for which allowances must be made in the multicultural class-room (see p.150).

Physical contact between children

I have found that there is always considerably more physical contact between the children in a multicultural school than between those who attend a school comprised entirely of indigenous children. This of course is understandable — if the children cannot make themselves understood with words, they will resort to physically handling each other which may lead to disciplinary problems and misunderstanding (see p.85). The frequent contacts and sometimes perpetual touching or pulling result in a series of complaints. 'He hit me', 'He pushed me', 'He took the spade without asking!'

Every summer term in my present school 'gang play' develops in the playground in spite of many varied efforts to prevent it, and more often than not the nucleus of each 'gang' is composed of one particular nationality however much we try to overcome or avoid such divisions.

The sensitive control of physical contacts in a multicultural school is one of the most difficult things to achieve, and, once again, there is no clear-cut answer.

Between the ages of four and seven all children are making and working out for themselves tremendous social adjustments, and when, in addition to this, they have to overcome language and cultural difficulties, we must expect and allow for certain strong disagreements. There will be pushing and snatching, hitting and grabbing; there will also be the reverse . 'I don't want to hold hands with her, she's coloured, she smells.'

Prejudice

Prejudice is sometimes prevalent in the infant school for a variety of reasons, and teachers must be prepared for it.

Adults often assume that such prejudice only develops among older children and should rarely exist in an infant school where surely the children are unaware of differences and just accept each other without any preconceived opposition. As an inexperienced teacher, I too had imagined that infant children were too young to concern themselves with any form of racial segregation, but I was sadly mistaken.

My first realisation of the problem occurred when Angela, a six-year-old West Indian asked if she could stay indoors at playtime because she was not allowed to join in the games with the other children as she had a brown face. The following day I sent her out as usual, but I stayed and watched at a distance. The children pushed her to the wall and then chanted together. 'She's got a brown face, she's got a brown face, don't play with Angela, she's got a brown face.' I shall always remember Angela, she was a bright-eyed, attractive girl and the first child in my experience to paint someone in her own dark colouring — she chose to illustrate Christ feeding the five thousand, and she gave Him a brown face.

We must, of course, get this matter in its right perspective. Many children do accept each other quite naturally whatever culture they belong to, without any obvious feeling of resentment or restraint. Friendships develop between children of different races and their parents accept this gladly. It is to be expected that children who speak a particular language, live in the same road, eat similar food and whose parents are related or friends will automatically group together, and thus a natural bond develops between the children of one particular nationality. Even so, many adults with whom I speak find it hard to believe me when I tell them that some five-year-old children are already conditioned to despising and rejecting their peers from other races before they enter school, and without knowing why, retaliate in a harmful and hurtful way as soon as they meet children of differing physique. There are various experiences which illustrate the way in which adults' attitudes can influence those of a child, but I do not wish to dwell upon them. A few examples may, however, help make the inexperienced teacher aware of the subtleties of this problem.

One January the heating in the school failed and all the parents had to be notified that the school could not be re-opened. Many parents were informed of the situation by telephone, but where this was not possible members of the staff visited the homes. The house in which one of the West Indian families lived was empty, and so the teacher asked the neighbour if she could tell the parents what had happened on their return. 'Oh no!' was the reply, 'They are coloured.' The only children who arrived at the school on the following morning were the two children from that West Indian family.

An elderly Asian grandfather was pushing his grandchild on a swing

in the local recreation ground. An English child sat on the neighbouring swing and seeing her inability to reach any height, the grandfather
turned and gave her a push. Immediately the English mother ran to
him and accused him of interfering with her child — for months the
old man was unable to return to the recreation ground.

A Ugandan Asian friend of mine is often wakened by noises through
her letter box at night, pestered with indecent telephone calls and
sometimes abused in the streets. If she does not take her milk indoors
immediately, it is removed. She is a highly educated person with a
charm, grace and kindness which exceeds my understanding.

When shopping with groups of children, my staff have sometimes
felt very conscious of the hostile attitude towards the coloured children expressed through small, but clearly defined remarks, and
although 99% of the people go out of their way to be kind and helpful, it is the hurtful comments of the 1% which unfortunately remain
in the children's memories.

Similar discrimination in the reverse creeps in as the 'immigrant'
community increases and becomes established. Trespassing and rubbish
dumping on other people's property are often the source of parochial
friction, and in one or two extreme cases fights have ensued.

Discrimination does not exist exclusively between dark and fair
skinned people — 'black and white'. West Indian children referring
to Asian families have told me that 'We don't speak to them — they're
coloured' and vice versa.

Where adult prejudices exist the children will have similar pre-con-
ceived ideas and attitudes, but it is interesting and encouraging to see
how often they change their opinions quite naturally once they have
formed their own relationships in school. How well I remember
watching two Greek and Turkish Cypriot boys working together on
a clay model ship, while their adult relations and friends stormed at
each other in protest marches and displayed antagonistic slogans
outside the school gate.

Alan was a new boy, he was English and six years of age when he
joined us. His mother, an enlightened social worker, had chosen to
send him to our multicultural school and was interested to hear his
comments after the first day. 'And how is the new school?' she asked.
'Well,' replied Alan thoughtfully, 'it's great, but it's very funny. The
children speak quite differently and . . . Mummy, if I'd been born in
Letchworth, would I have had a brown face too?'

Physical differences between the peers in a multicultural school

do pose problems, but my advice is never try to hide them, do not
sweep them under the desk! Talk about colour, the different shades
of complexion, the different hair textures, and compare the colour
of eyes. If you find a child trying to scrub off his brown colouring,
boost his morale all you can, and make him realise that very many
people with pale skins spend hours trying to turn them brown. Discuss the climate of the countries from which the 'brown' children
come and do everything you can to make them, and their parents,
proud of their inheritance — they have a right to be!

We are all formed differently as individuals and what a blessing
this is. Let the children see that you do not want them to look alike
— they are different, and they should be proud and not ashamed to
be different. I was speaking to a group of adults on this subject, and,
knowing that some were not English, I wondered how they would
react to my comments. Afterwards an Italian nun came up to me and
said, 'Oh! I was so pleased to hear you say that you appreciated the
differences in people of other nationalities. I cannot laugh like English
people — my laugh is so big and loud; I cannot easily drink coffee
like you either, in tiny sips, I drink it in one long gulp!'

Try to help the children from their very early contacts in school
to see one another's differences in a positive way, and to accept and
to respect them alongside learning to conform to a general, socially
desirable code of behaviour.

The morning assembly is a time when I occasionally talk about these
differences if I feel the need is there, and sometimes invite a parent
from a minority group to help me. We point out to the children the
difference in the colour of our hands and arms and then lead on to the
fact that we both are as important as each other in the work we do and
the friends we make. One West Indian mother who has assisted me in
this way is a nurse, and the children are able to appreciate the medical
help which she gives to others, help which I cannot offer. Recently my
deputy head's husband was a patient in the same hospital where this
mother works, and her six-year-old daughter Cheryl urged her to visit
him. This she gladly did during her 'off duty' hours, and Cheryl and
the deputy head were able to share with the children the pleasure
which was given as a result.

Although I have referred in some detail to the difficulties of physical contacts between peers in multicultural schools because they are
the ones which may cause problems, I must emphasise that in many
cases children socialise quickly and well without any form of biased

prejudice — so much depends on the child's own temperament and personality.

Summary

The following list is one which was originally compiled for students and has proved helpful — it summarises briefly the main practical points to which we have referred.

Reminders for teachers admitting non-English speaking children to their classes

(1) Routine is essential. Everything has to be learned by watching.

(2) Each non-English speaking child should be given a place of his own, and a box or drawer where he can keep his belongings. A sense of security is essential.

(3) Begin by giving the non-English speaking child something definite to do, an activity in which he has shown an interest, a simple task which he is able to enjoy, and in which he can achieve a measure of success. Do not be disturbed if he sits and watches, but make sure he is not watching because he does not know how to play with the material in front of him.

(4) Be definite in your instructions. Demonstrate to the child how to sort the shapes or thread the beads.

(5) Clay, dough, even paint will often at first be avoided by children of minority groups. Do not worry about this. Given time and encouragement the non-English speaking child will experiment with all the new materials.

(6) Remember that situations requiring language, such as playing with others in the home corner or sharing the sand or bricks, can be the most frustrating ones. A non-English speaking child may be distressed, even deeply depressed by his inability to take an active part.

(7) If the non-English speaking child wants to draw and 'write' a great deal at first, let him. If he prefers pencils to crayons during his first days at school, allow him to work with a pencil, but always leave the crayons near by.

(8) As far as possible avoid situations in which the non-English speaking child is unable to participate.

(9) Use visual aids for stories, or give the non-English speaking child illustrations to study while you are reading or telling a story (if no other facilities are available).

(10) When the non-English speaking child copies pictures and word cards, ensure that the pictures are significant to him, and are introducing a vocabulary which will be useful to him in the near future. (Words like 'wig', 'ink', 'kit' are not needed as vitally as 'sit', 'run', etc!)

(11) It may help to write down all the things which a non-English speaking child can do as well as an English speaking child, e.g. performing simple practical tasks such as matching, sorting, giving out the milk, etc.

(12) Then write down the things which a non-English speaking child cannot do, e.g. talking to other children in the home corner; discussing past events or stories or TV programmes or news from home; understanding instructions, requests, explanations or stories; manipulating apparatus like jig-saw puzzles (due to lack of experience with toys of this sort).

(13) Notice what the non-English speaking child likes best as a classroom activity. Encourage this and develop it.

(14) If the child sits in one place all day, periodically change the equipment on the table before him.

(15) Avoid activities in which he might become frustrated or overwhelmed.
(See also Garvie 1976, p.36.)

Special points to remember when admitting non-English speaking children to the classroom

(1) Non-English speaking children will always be behind the other children when instructions are given — to go to the door, to line up, to wash their hands, to put their things away, for instance.

(2) Non-English speaking children will be bewildered about what is going to happen next when the routine changes.

(3) In every situation in which the English language plays a part, the English speaking children are likely to dominate; the non-English speaking children, therefore, need constant help and encouragement.

(4) Do not always place the non-English speaking child with groups of less able children.

(5) Children from minority groups have possibly not been used to playing with the materials provided in school. They may never have used clay, paint or dough, and may be afraid of soiling their clothes.

(6) Parents of minority group children often expect them to read and write at school, but not necessarily to move around and 'play'.

(7) Parents of non-English speaking children may not understand work or messages which are sent home.

(8) Children from overseas and different cultures cannot adapt overnight, but with patience, forethought, help and understanding will achieve a great deal during their first year in school, and contribute much to the class.

11 The language group

A positive place of learning

The teacher who is responsible for the language group must of course be well qualified to carry out this work, and by well qualified I mean someone who not only has a sound knowledge of how to teach English as a second language, but also has experience and an awareness of the needs and development of young children, particularly in the acquisition of the mother tongue. A person who is qualified to teach English as a second language should be very conscious of the sentence structure and vocabulary which she uses and introduces to the children. She should have her own resources of materials, books, equipment, games and activities and, because she does not have to consider the needs of the indigenous children, she should be able to concentrate her energies on producing or acquiring new materials and attending relevant courses or lectures (Garvie 1976).

The language area must be a *positive* place of learning. The children are not simply withdrawn from the classroom because they are failures who cannot cope with the situation there, they are taken out in order to do something special — this attitude is essential and must permeate throughout the whole school. The teacher should be a person who can establish a good and positive relationship with not only the E2L children but also the indigenous children and, of course, the other members of staff.

For many years I have been fortunate enough to have teachers of this calibre in my school, and in order to clarify what I mean by a 'positive place of learning' I must refer to a few of the activities in which they and the E2L children have been involved. It must be emphasised that throughout these activities and projects, controlled sentence structures and vocabulary were carefully introduced, reinforced and extended both in the general conversation and during the follow-up work when games, songs, rhymes, pictures and other materials were used (Garvie 1976). Because of the children's involvement in the activities, the new language being learnt was a *living* language where concepts were experienced and became meaningful.

The language group at Hillshott

The language group at Hillshott meets in a hut adjoining the school. Without this room it would be impossible to carry out the teaching of English in the way we do; there should be far more concern over the appalling cramped and overcrowded corners in which many teachers of English as a second language have to work.

The room has been furnished with basic equipment similar to that used in the classrooms, i.e. sand, water, home corner, paint, clay, bricks, etc., plus a cooker. Books, puzzles and mathematic equipment are selected carefully with the needs of immigrant and E2L children in mind.

The children who attend the language class are grouped according to their ability to speak English, although older children who have recently arrived in England may be helped separately from the younger ones. The groups average approximately eight children. Those who have no or very little English will attend for an hour each day, others on alternate days according to their needs.

In our particular circumstances we have found that Indian, Pakistani, Yugoslav, Italian, Greek, Turkish, Chinese and any other children for whom English is a completely strange language, have fitted in well together, although they do require help in slightly different ways regarding pronunciation.

West Indian children very often benefit from this group work, both socially and in connection with their language development. Sometimes they have been included with the Asian children, and at other times we have grouped them separately — so much depends on the individual child and his requirements.

When our language class was first introduced it catered for the needs of several nationalities; during recent years, however, the major part of our language work has been with Pakistani and Indian children, and the following examples are taken from the activities and methods which we have used with the latter group of children.

Language arising from experience

During the first days when the children are given time to settle in, the teacher observes and listens, and it will not be long before an opportunity arises in which she can easily and naturally introduce the English language.

Starting points often arise from the children's work, their paintings or models. They frequently discuss the activities in their own language, but the time soon comes when the child wants to share his work with an adult, and is keen and anxious to communicate with the teacher. The teacher then introduces the appropriate English vocabulary as far as possible, and begins gradually to build and extend it from the child's own point of interest.

English language is continually being introduced into the every-day occurrences within the group. During the first week of one term an Indian girl was crying and the teacher rolled a cylindrical brick across the floor to attract her attention; immediately the other children gathered around and, fascinated, they also rolled other cylindrical bricks — the language work began. 'It is rolling, look, the brick is rolling to Kuldip.' Throughout the following two weeks the children made a collection of objects that rolled. This led on to wheels and they spent time examining and making models and pictures of vehicles. The children looked at the cars in the playground and went out to watch the traffic in the streets; they discussed trains, buses, carts, bicycles — anything with wheels. This is one example of a successful starting point, especially as it involved cars — the Indian children in our area love cars, and 'car' is a word they use and understand.

The teacher does not, however, just sit back and wait for appropriate opportunities to arise. She plans and prepares her work with tremendous foresight and care, placing in the room equipment which will stimulate a specific vocabulary and give her the opportunity to teach definite language patterns.

One of the most successful ways of doing this is to introduce starting points which are common to everyone, for example food and clothing — both offer endless opportunities for language development and experience. They also incorporate an important aspect of the teacher's work, that of creating a link with the children's home and family life.

Food

In a previous chapter I mentioned having cooking utensils and 'make believe' food familiar to the children of different nationalities in the classroom home corner. This can be fully extended in the language area. Meals can be discussed, tables set, shops visited and recipes cooked and eaten. Among many, many other varied menus, our children have made toast, boiled and fried eggs, cooked chapatis and pancakes, made porridge and soup, jam, tea, cakes, biscuits and pies. I mention these items because each one was used to explain a particular point.

Toast. The children in this group were six years of age and had already experienced one year in school. The teacher had noticed that they did not know what toast was and so they made some, and when they saw it they referred to it as 'burnt bread'. As I watched two Indian children spreading the slices, I noted carefully the language which the teacher was introducing. 'Look, Charanjit is putting butter on the toast, she is spreading butter on the toast. Harmesh is putting butter on the toast, he is spreading butter on the toast. What are they doing? She is spreading butter on the toast. He is spreading butter on the toast. They are spreading butter on the toast. How many pieces have they spread with butter?' The toast was then spread with honey.

Eggs. Many of the children in the language group are vegetarians, but they enjoy eating eggs which are, of course, nourishing. As the English variations of cooking them were unknown, two older sisters were invited to come and help fry, boil and poach!

Chapatis and pancakes. The older sisters were invited into school to show us how to make chapatis. The value of this experience was not simply the activity, but also the interchange of two languages and the opportunity for the children to watch the adult members of their community demonstrating to the teacher (and the school cook and headmistress) how to make something from their own culture and share the enjoyment together.

During the following week pancakes were made. Once again the older sisters were present, but this time they learnt to cook the English recipe. The occasion was followed up by the story of 'The Big Pancake' told first in Punjabi by one of the sisters and later in simple English by the teacher using illustrations.

Porridge. Porridge is often made with the younger groups in the language class because the story of 'The Three Bears' is such an appropriate one to tell, and a tale the children love. The language is simple and repetitive and the children soon learn to join in. Deliberately creating lumps and putting too much salt into the porridge gives much enjoyment, and 'too hot' and 'too cold' are expressive terms when accompanied by first-hand experience in this way! The role play of father, mother or baby bear is much more interesting when the porridge is genuine, even if at the end some is left to waste.

Jam. The making of blackberry jelly occurred when we realised that many of the Indian parents and children did not know what blackberries were. Living, as they do, within easy reach of the countryside the older children were taken out to pick blackberries. Some of the fruit was eaten raw, some was stewed and eaten and the remainder was made into jam — each child eventually taking a little home.

Tea and cakes. Cakes are often made by the children, but the most important occasions for cooking them are those when their mothers or grandmothers are invited to a tea party. The visitors are sometimes asked to bring a small contribution of their own native sweetmeats, and different recipes are tasted and shared. Tea or coffee is also served and phrases such as 'Please would you pass the cakes to . . . ', 'May I have . . . ' or 'Would you like . . . ' are practised.

Biscuits. Biscuits incorporating geometrical and animal shapes or an assortment of other designs are popular — one of the favourites being gingerbread men followed by the story of 'The Gingerbread Man' told in both Punjabi and English.

Soup. Turnip soup always heralds 'The Tale of the Enormous Turnip', but even when the teacher has prepared something as definite as this, she must be ready to adapt if there is a sudden turn in events.

On one occasion the children added other vegetables to the turnip soup. They had visited the greengrocer's and purchased an interesting assortment of vegetables which they first handled and displayed before finally cutting, peeling, cooking and eating them. Unfortunately the peas remained hard and so the teacher told the children to take them out of the soup and put them on the edge of their plates. 'Edge', that was a new word, so while the children ate their soup, and carefully removed the peas, they discussed not only vegetables but 'edges' — the edge of the table, the edge of the chair, etc. One never knows what new words will unexpectedly arise and catch the children's imagination. 'Edge' was repeatedly heard and spoken that day and many edges touched and felt. The language teacher should have the time and facilities to follow up useful digressions wherever possible.

Pies. Our children have enjoyed making an assortment of pies and it all started through a visit to a vegetable garden. Following the visit, which was made in order to see and touch growing vegetables, the children were told the story of 'Peter Rabbit'. They benefited from the language (Mr McGregor looked *under* the flower pots, *behind* the wheelbarrow, *in* the watering can) and the older children enjoyed 'acting' the story at one of the morning assemblies, but there was a phrase which proved puzzling — 'Peter's father was put in a pie.' The children did not know what a pie was, and so they made one (vegetable, not rabbit!). This was followed by several nursery rhymes — 'Little Jack Horner', 'Simple Simon' and 'Sing a Song of Sixpence', and when Christmas was approaching, mince pies were a very acceptable addition.

Occasionally a few of the older children have prepared and cooked a simple meal. The children involved were those who had had two to three years in the school and could speak and understand English sufficiently well to cope with the general classroom activities. It is important that children who have reached this stage are not left devoid of any extra help or encouragement. The aim of the language teacher is that the immigrant and E2L children should be able to speak 'English' English, and it is important to perfect their use of the second language as much as possible. It is also important for them not to feel that they are being continually withdrawn from their classroom because they are considered to be less able than the other children especially when, according to their own estimation, they are comprehending satisfactorily.

Special activities are, therefore, planned for these children so that they look forward to participating and, because by this stage they are thoroughly secure working with the language teacher, they can accept her corrections of their speech providing she makes them tactfully.

One morning a group of these children cooked the caretaker his breakfast. They fried bacon and egg and made tea and toast. Much discussion and valuable language work took place, but one conversation remained uppermost in my mind during the few minutes I happened to be in the room.

The caretaker opened the jar of marmalade.
>TEACHER: 'Children, what is in the jar?'
>CHILD: 'Jam.'
>TEACHER: 'No, it's like jam, but we call it marmalade; what do we call it?'
>CHILDREN: 'Marmalade.'
>TEACHER: 'Look, can you see what it's made of?'
>The children were unable to guess the contents.
>TEACHER: 'It's made with oranges. Look, I've got an orange in my pocket.'
>The teacher produced an orange (good preparation and planning!).
>TEACHER: 'Now, marmalade is made from the outside of an orange. What do you think we call the outside of an orange?'

CHILD: 'Shell.' (They had been examining nuts on a previous day.)
TEACHER: 'No, good try though, nuts have a shell but oranges have some-
      thing that we have.'
The children were unable to guess.
TEACHER: 'We call it the skin. Now, when we make marmalade, we have to
      take the skin off the orange. We *peel* it off. What do we do?'
CHILD: 'Peel it off.'
TEACHER: 'Now, watch while I peel the skin off. When we peel the skin off
      like this it changes its name — we call it peel. Can you see the
      orange peel in the marmalade?'
A brief discussion followed, then a child turned and touched the outside of
the loaf of bread.
TEACHER: 'Now, the outside of the loaf of bread has a special name too, does
      anyone know what it is?'
CHILD: 'Shell.'
TEACHER: 'No.'
CHILD: 'Skin.'
TEACHER: 'No.'
CHILD: 'Peel.'
TEACHER: 'No, I'll tell you — we call it crust.'
CHILDREN: 'Crust.'

Clothes

Clothes are a common source of interest and create not only opportunities for lively conversation, but provide an insight into culture
and custom.

Children in the infant school love new clothes and they enjoy
touching and commenting on the teacher's garments in no uncertain
terms. A child who cannot understand what you are saying usually
knows if you are admiring her outfit, and this goes for boys too! The
mothers, who often take such a pride in dressing their children,
appreciate a teacher's obvious delight at the clothes which either they
or their children are wearing.

Conversation concerning this topic arises naturally because of the
need to help children to dress and undress in the infant school. Hang-
ing up and caring for clothes is important, and stressing the need for
suitable clothing according to the weather is often necessary.

Sometimes there is good reason for developing one aspect in particular, and an opportunity to do this occurred when the teacher
needed a new hat to wear at a Christening service. Indian children,
like all children, are fascinated with hats, especially the girls whose
mothers have never possessed or worn one. A hat shop was erected

in the corner of the language room, and hats poured in from all quarters of the school. (The indigenous children are often included in helping to provide material and they always like to know what is going on and are eager to participate if invited — an important attribute to creating a positive image of the language group.) The children wore and played endlessly with the wide selection of hats, and words such as 'helmet', 'cap', 'peak', 'brim', 'crown', 'bridesmaid', 'fireman', 'postman', etc. slipped into their vocabulary, but the project did not end there — this was only the beginning.

The following week the teacher went to buy the new hat and took eight of the Indian girls to the millinery department of a large store in a neighbouring town. There they watched her trying on and finally purchasing a hat of their choice! Later on the teacher showed the children photographs of the Christening and, of course, lively discussions ensued; the following day some of the Indian children arrived at school with wedding photographs. Finally an Indian grandmother accompanied by relations and friends, brought a most beautiful sari into the hall for a morning assembly. This was much admired by everyone and the children (minority-group and indigenous) measured it, then we watched silently while the grandmother dressed the deputy head in her attractive garment.

Homes and houses

Homes are, of course, a familiar concept to everyone but variations amongst them can stimulate both useful and essential language work.

A doll's house is a helpful piece of equipment in the language room and from this starting point the teacher can go on to visit homes with the children. Neighbouring houses, flats and bungalows can be observed from the exterior, and then, if possible, arrangements should be made for the children to see inside some of them. The school governors can be of great assistance in this way, and our E2L children have spent some very happy and valuable mornings being given a guided tour of inspection by one of the governors round his or her home. This gives the host or hostess a little insight into the language difficulties encountered by the children and ways in which they can be helped. It can also help to form and further the link with the governing body and the work within the school.

The teacher's home is naturally an obvious one to visit, and it is important that homes of the children's nationalities should be included.

Some of the people living near our school have been most welcoming, and in particular one lady who has a collection of shining horse brasses which intrigue the children.

Follow-up work in the classroom will involve painting, creative work, songs, games, flannel or cellograph pictures, illustrations, and stories, and once again cooking may also be included. Stories frequently used in connection with houses are 'The Three Pigs', 'The Old Woman in the Vinegar Bottle', 'The Three Bears' and 'Hansel and Gretel'. The children have made ingenious Hansel and Gretel houses, and learning words such as 'tiles', 'chimney', 'door step', 'door knob', 'letter box', 'window sill', 'drain pipe', etc. can be so much more inviting when you are creating them from biscuits, liquorice all-sorts and icing sugar.

It does help to concentrate on one room at a time and to draw out from the children what they do in those rooms at home, if indeed they have the rooms in question. Many of the children are cramped in one or two rooms, and have to learn the concept of a kitchen or bedroom as separate entities. Others will have knowledge and experience of furniture but name them incorrectly; for example, a 'pillow' (cushion), an 'eating table' (dining room table).

As the children share these experiences the teacher ensures that the same phrases are being reinforced, the same language patterns repeated and the same words used in different situations. Thus the children gradually build not only an English vocabulary connected with houses, but a meaningful concept of homes — their own and other people's.

The language teacher is encouraged to take her children out even at a moment's notice if she feels the need for them to share in a particular experience. It may be just for a walk along the road to look at trees, flowers, doors, windows, people or traffic; it may be a visit to the shops or market (there are always things to buy) or a garage or the station.

Another important experience is to use the telephone. If a suitable person telephones me when a child (indigenous or E2L) is in my room I hand the receiver over — and on other occasions children make calls for a variety of reasons. It is good for them occasionally to communicate through language alone without any form of visual support, and of course the opportunity to dial a number and use the telephone is a valuable experience in itself.

The school and the language group

During some of my visits to other schools I have noticed the non-English speaking children being withdrawn from the classroom and then given books to look at or word and picture games in which to participate, involving the names of a wide variety of comparatively unimportant objects. As I watch the children using equipment in these situations, I become more and more concerned about the remoteness of the vocabulary which is introduced during what could be such valuable periods of concentrated language development.

The two pressing needs for a non-English speaking child in school are to adjust socially and to learn the relevant vocabulary which will enable him both to understand and be understood within the immediate environment. It is essential for the language teacher to work very, very closely with the class teachers and to reinforce the general work within the school as much as possible.

Links between teachers

At the beginning of every morning the teacher who takes the language group in our school is in the cloakroom to meet the children alongside the class teacher and occasionally she spends part of the day in the classroom watching the E2L children in this particular environment. All the teachers continually exchange information with her, asking her to give additional help with a certain word or piece of equipment.

There was a time when the BBC music and movement programmes on the radio began with 'Find a space', and although many of the E2L children enjoyed the programme and could appreciate the music without difficulty, they were completely lost by that opening phrase and often bewildered by the other children suddenly rushing all over the hall. The language teacher heard about this and she spent a considerable amount of time explaining, discussing and re-enacting 'space' with the E2L children. She also incorporated other words such as 'under', 'over', 'round', 'beside', 'high', 'low', 'in' and 'out' which many non-English speaking children find hard to learn (Garvie 1976).

If the class teacher notices that an E2L child is having particular difficulty in fastening his clothes, holding a pencil, using scissors, matching colours or shapes, completing puzzles, etc., she does not have to worry unduly about finding the considerable additional time required to give him the extra assistance he needs in the classroom. The language teacher is made aware of the problem and she will then try to help the child in the smaller group situation and introduce and practise the relevant vocabulary at the same time.

The language teacher occasionally also assists during the period when the reception classes have PE. This gives her an insight into the children's physical abilities, she can also repeat or reinforce the class teacher's instructions and give practical help when necessary.

Both the class teachers and the language teacher listen constantly for the mistakes and misunderstandings which continually arise — they then compare notes and decide how best to help the child. Tape recordings are made regularly with individual children both in English and in their own language. These conversations are often based on the week's work in the language group, and the recordings are carefully analysed. This enables us to note syntactical discrepancies and to detect breakdowns in the child's comprehension which we might otherwise miss.

Errors may be clear-cut grammatical mistakes or mispronunciations, but very often they are a mixed confusion and misplacement of the English vocabulary. I have referred previously to the 'washing string'.

An Indian girl, who could speak and understand English reasonably well, wrote in her news book, 'My Mummy hung the washing on the washing string.' The language teacher was told and she spent several sessions on 'lines', 'strings', 'ribbons', 'cotton', 'belts', 'laces', 'thread', 'wool', etc., in fact anything which might be confused with string, and she tried to teach the children the difference between them and the purposes for which they were used.

Another example which caused confusion for some children was the difference between 'go backwards' and 'come back' — again the language teacher spent time in moving the children accordingly and helping them to differentiate between 'back', 'backwards', 'come back' and 'backing'.

Intonation

It is sometimes very difficult for an immigrant or an E2L child to hear the difference between particular sounds which do not occur in his mother tongue, for example 'v' and 'w'. He may appear to be listening but this does not necessarily ensure that he is consciously hearing the sound in the way the teacher intends. In order to help children to develop their ability to listen, suitable games should be introduced — for example, an adult or another child hides behind a screen and makes different sounds, (or alternatively a variety of sounds are recorded and played back) for the children to recognise.

Another way of helping children to listen and reproduce the rhythm of the English language is to tap out phrases and sentences with a stick or musical instrument. Repeating sentences in different ways, varying the emphasis and volume is also helpful, for example: '*I* have lost my pencil; I *have* lost my pencil; I have *lost* my pencil; I have lost *my* pencil; I have lost my *pencil;* I have lost my pencil? I have lost my pencil! [loudly] ; I have lost my pencil [sadly] ; I have lost my pencil [whispered].

One valuable source of information concerning the needs of the immigrant and E2L children is the contribution made by the English welfare helpers in the school. They work with assorted groups of children, for example playing games or cooking with them. These helpers are in the unique position of listening to the children who are learning English conversing with other children in small numbers, and they often see a completely different side of a child or notice a particular difficulty which only comes to light in these situations.

Reading

When the children who are learning to speak English are anxious to have reading books, the language teacher ensures that they have an understanding of the situations which will arise in the first few books of our reading scheme before the children are faced with the printed page. In the first instance she will give opportunities for the children to experience the situation as far as possible for themselves, without any reference to the books, so that they will fully understand the concepts behind the story and not develop the pseudo-reading techniques to which I referred earlier. For example, for the phrase 'I can ride', the children will discuss and experience riding on different vehicles.

Our Asian assistant also discusses in the children's mother tongue the English words and phrases they are reading. This is very important because, as the following examples show, these children can so easily slightly misunderstand a simple remark. A boy read 'Grandfather looks after the children.' He assured the assistant that he understood what this meant, but when 'looks after' was discussed his explanation was 'watching the children with a smile' (as depicted in the illustration) – he had no idea that 'looking after' something involved any further action such as 'taking care of it'. Another boy described 'look out' as 'staring', and a third showed bewilderment when he read the sentence 'The plane was on fire' because the flames were coming out of the cockpit: 'Why' he asked 'does it say that, when the plane is not on the fire?'

Both the language teacher and the assistant watch for any sight or hearing defects, as these may prove difficult to detect in children who do not understand what is being said.

The class teachers are very much aware of the activities in progress in the language room and records are kept of the rhymes, songs and stories to which the children have listened and in which they have joined.

Behaviour

Problems of behaviour are discussed and it is a help to a class teacher to have the language teacher's support concerning the difficulties. I personally find that having someone on the staff who can give her time solely to the needs of these children is a tremendous relief, knowing the length of time it can take to sort out some simple matter concerning dinner money, a lost item or a disagreement. The question of time is such a vital one in a multicultural school when communication takes so much longer, and one is either forced to leave a child to fend for himself and sort out his own problems, or ensure that there is someone who can make time to work through the complex barriers of communication and reach a satisfactory conclusion.

Assemblies

The language teacher gives me tremendous support in this particular aspect of our school activities. Visual aids are used in many of our assemblies and the gathering is made as informal and interesting as possible. It is not easy to know how much the children who have difficulty in understanding the English language can comprehend, especially when they are listening in a crowd. Sometimes these children leave early, but often they remain until the end, and it is surprising how much information they do glean and how much enthusiasm they show. After assembly the language teacher quickly runs through any special points of interest or importance, and reinforces what has been said, incorporating an occasional outing if necessary.

The assemblies are mainly based on basic moral teaching and all the children attend — our Hindu member of staff also participates. Sometimes reference is made to Christianity and a suitable story from the Bible may be told — this particularly applies to Christmas — but we also include simple stories from the other religions represented, and thus obtain a glimpse into each other's culture, and a little more understanding of each other's way of life.

Future events

One very important aspect of the language teacher's work is to prepare the children for future events. I have already referred to the fact that it is extremely difficult to recall the past or speak about the future to children who cannot understand English (see pp. 118—20).

At the beginning of the term the language teacher notes in her diary any future events which will involve her children; it might be a visit from the school doctor or dentist, the audiologist or optician, the health visitor, the road safety representative or the crossing patrol, the school photographer, a group of musicians or the piano tuner — anyone whom the children may suddenly have to meet. During the days before their arrival the language teacher tries to ensure that the children in her group know a little about them and what to expect. She may simply use a few illustrations and discuss them with the children, or she may turn the home corner into a hospital or dental surgery.

The children are also prepared for any future activity which may be new and confusing to them. Before they undress for their first PE lesson or splash in the paddling pool, they are taken to watch other children participating in the activity.

Time is spent in preparing the children for simple celebrations such as the birthday candles which are lit every Monday in the hall (many of the Indian children are unaccustomed to celebrating their birthdays) or the festivals — Harvest, Diwali and Christmas.

Prior to a recent Harvest festival the E2L children visited an allotment, a small garden and a walled kitchen garden in a private estate in order to study vegetables. They noticed which vegetables grew under the ground, and they felt and handled those above ground. They fingered beans, and stroked pumpkins, tasted tomatoes and pulled up carrots. When the Harvest produce was displayed they were able to recognise and speak about all the varieties of vegetables which had been brought.

The class outings always cause a sense of excitement and usually inspire some interesting activity both before and after the event. The language teacher knows where the children are going and she nearly always accompanies them, joining each class in turn. Prior to their visits she explains with visual aids where they are going and what to expect.

One year we felt sure that a particular group of children would not be provided with a practical and nourishing packed lunch because of the inability to communicate with the parents and explain what was required. (We did not have a suitable interpreter at the time.) The language teacher, therefore, planned a mini-outing two weeks before-hand. The children went to the shops and purchased the ingredients for a picnic. Returning to school, they made sandwiches and prepared the fruit, etc., then, packing the food carefully into suitable bags or satchels, they went off on a fishing expedition. Two fish were caught (by the same boy, which was rather unfortunate) and afterwards the food was appropriately consumed and a good day was had by all. When the time came for the class outings, all the children brought a suitable packed lunch.

The language teacher has found it helpful to have another adult in her room, not only to give additional assistance with the children, but also to help explain something visually. Questions and answers, commands and responses can be put into practice and then imitated by the children. For many years all the welfare helpers in our school were English. They were attached to the language group in turn — a year at a time — and they proved to be a tremendous support to the teacher. I felt, however, that it was essential for us to have an adult on our staff who could understand and speak to the Asian children in their own language. When a vacancy arose I was fortunate to be able to appoint a Ugandan Asian who could not only converse in the children's languages, but also write them. Her qualities and quali-fications complement those of the teacher, and together they play a major part not only in teaching English as a second language, but also in the social aspect of our school and the immigrant community.

Adverse attitudes

Sometimes language groups and centres are overlooked and considered unnecessary by experienced teachers. This may be the fault of the language centre, but so much specialised language work depends on the co-operation of all the staff concerned. I have repeatedly emphasised that the language teacher must be qualified for, and experienced with, the age group with whom she is working, and both she and the class teacher must be ready to accept advice and help from each other. I have known a fully equipped language centre to be spurned by teachers who, because of their long experience in the profession, consider that they can give the child the help he requires in the classroom without the assistance of anyone else. This particularly applies to infant teachers, and children are prevented from receiving correct second language teaching until they are older and unable to cope with their work; by then it is often too late for them to receive the full benefit of a language group.

Other teachers have failed to make good use of withdrawal groups and classes held within the school. In certain instances there has been a lack of liaison between class teachers and the language specialist; head teachers have been known to oppose language groups in their schools; fear of being accused of segregation by the 'immigrant' community, or favouritism by the indigenous parents, have been the reasons for this in some cases.

It is important for the parents of non-English speaking children to fully understand why their children are being withdrawn, and to re-assure them that the reason for doing so is to help them learn English more quickly, and not because the children are retarded in any way. The indigenous parents usually appreciate non-English speaking children leaving the class for a short while during which time their own children are not held back by language difficulties.

It is imperative that in all multicultural schools a good sound curriculum is maintained for the English speaking children, and that they do not suffer academically because of the language problems confronting other children. It is as important for English speaking children to be released from any pressures of delay, misunderstanding or frustrated behaviour, as it is for non-English speaking children to be released from the pressures of the classroom.

The language room should be a place where the immigrant and E2L children are helped to adjust from one culture to another without losing respect for their own. Language is only part of the culture — a major part — but etiquette, clothing, religion, food and many other different aspects in the cultures must be recognised and sensitively integrated into the work of the language teacher.

With young children language stems from experiencing, investigating and discovering, from moving, sharing, touching and talking, but the environment must be the right one, and the teacher qualified to create and develop it.

A large measure of attention has to be paid . . . to the educational needs of the children labelled 'immigrant'. Obviously what is needed is as sharp a measure as possible of these special educational needs. An immigrant child does not present problems to a school simply because he is an immigrant child . . .

No child should be expected to cast off the language and culture of the home as he crosses the school threshold, nor to live and act as though school and home represent two totally separate and different cultures which have to be kept firmly apart. The curriculum should reflect many elements of that part of his life which a child lives outside school . . .

For children with language difficulties it is essential that for a short period every day a teacher should sit with individuals or small groups and talk with them. (Department of Education and Science 1976, pp.234, 286, 292.)

Social welfare and the need for an interpreter

The welfare of the immigrant and E2L children would suffer considerably if we did not have two responsible and caring members of staff who make time to delve into, and solve, so many problems which, although outside the province of language teaching, have a tremendous bearing on the children's happiness, attitudes and progress. It is impossible to record many incidents, but the selected few illustrate the need to have (a) someone who is appointed specifically to help the E2L children, and (b) a responsible person who can speak and write the languages of the local minority groups as well as English.

In our particular situation, school letters are sent out in both English and Hindustani, and this has encouraged Asian parents to attend open evenings, and take a lively interest in other school functions. They now know what is happening and are eager to co-operate.

Medical forms have also been translated, although problems do continually arise concerning their completion prior to the examination. It is difficult for a school doctor to examine a child without a parent's consent, but our Asian assistant is usually able to unravel the numerous complications and misunderstandings.

R— had taken home three forms concerning medical examinations, none had been returned. The boy missed one appointment, and when a second opportunity came to see the doctor we were anxious for him and his mother to be present. The Asian assistant took a form to the

home, it was not returned. She called again and completed the form
which the mother had to sign with a cross. The medical examination
took place and the boy was found to have a diseased hip which will
involve years of hospital treatment. If our assistant had not persevered
in obtaining the form, and spoken the mother's language, the boy's
condition would have seriously deteriorated. It must be added that
the school medical officer is extremely helpful and co-operative in
such cases and would have responded to my request for advice concerning the child had I noticed a defect; nevertheless, parental consent
is necessary before any further steps can be taken or treatment given.

A doctor prescribed K—— with a bottle of medicine. K——'s mother,
unable to read the directions, administered it all during the course of
two days. She was then concerned about his reactions and contacted
the school. Our assistant discussed the matter with her, and sought
the necessary medical advice.

When children are taken ill during school hours, the Asian assistant
is able to telephone the parents either at home or at their place of
work, and, speaking to them in their own language, she can alleviate
their fears, explain the symptoms to the parents and advise them on
the precautions which should be taken. This is particularly helpful
when there has been an accident and hospital treatment is necessary.
A few years ago a case of typhoid occurred in the school, and how we
would have tackled the interviewing and endless questioning without
our interpreter, I do not know.

Children are kept away from school for a variety of reasons and
these can be investigated by the Asian assistant who is far more capable
of locating the cause of absence than an English attendance officer who
cannot speak the required language.

Once our assistant discovered that two of the Indian children were
in hospital. We went to visit them, and, although one had settled in
well, the other girl was fretting badly; she had been in hospital for a
week and the nurses were still under the impression that she could
not understand what was being said to her. We were able to assure
them that she spoke English fluently and should have no language
difficulty whatsoever.

Our Asian assistant is able to inform us about the diet which the
children are given at home and we are also aware of the children who
have to prepare their own meals, or even feed younger members of
the family. She can also answer the parents queries concerning school
meals and the provision of vegetarian food if desired.

An Indian mother appeared at the classroom door one morning
with a packet of cornflakes. Our assistant spoke to her and was asked
if the school could please give her boy his breakfast, as he was too
tired to get up and eat it! The assistant explained that we did not
have the facilities to do this even though the mother offered to return
with a plate and spoon. It was politely emphasised that we could not
give children breakfast, and suggested that in future the boy was sent
to bed earlier than eleven o'clock.

The Asian assistant is able to seek out information regarding the
hours of sleep which some of the children have — many of them (like
the indigenous children) appear to be overtired during the day. Some
share beds, others share rooms with adults or the television.

One of our children curled up on the floor and slept like an animal.
We discovered that he never went to bed until the television programmes had closed down and then, because he had no bed of his
own, he chose an adult member of the family to sleep with — it might
have been grandfather, father, mother, auntie or uncle.

Whenever we are concerned about a child in any way, whether it
be his physical, mental or emotional condition, it is so good to be
able to turn to our assistant, knowing that she will do all that is within
her power to answer our queries.

K—— , a boy aged five years who had begun to speak English, became
sullen and withdrawn. Neither the class nor language teacher could communicate with him and his work deteriorated. After two weeks, he
suddenly confided in the Asian assistant, who finally persuaded him to
tell her in his own language why he was unhappy. He explained that
his mother was dead, lying in bed with broken legs. The assistant
visited the house, but was prevented from entering by the father, who
assured her that all was well. Not satisfied, she crept unseen into the
house on the following day. The bedroom door was barricaded, but
eventually she gained admission and discovered the mother in a semi-
conscious condition having been beaten by her husband.

Medical help was sought and the case reported to the Social Services who regularly visited the family thereafter.

This incident made us very much aware of the fact that several
of the Asian mothers in our area were being treated in a similar way.
Unable to read, write or speak English, they did not know how to
obtain help or protection.

The language teacher and the assistant make a point of regularly
locating the children's parents. Sometimes they move without inform-

ing us, and frequently one or the other leaves for a temporary stay in the Punjab. New relations join the families and our assistant often tells me about a mother, aunt or grandmother who has recently arrived and is terrified to leave the house, sitting, possibly all day, with the curtains drawn. Such experiences must have some effect on the children.

Very, very occasionally there is a division in an Asian family, and the school is approached concerning the children. Our assistant was asked to represent the school in a meeting with a social worker and a family where the parents had been granted a divorce; there was a possibility of the children being placed into care. Fortunately, because of the assistant, it was discovered that the grandparents very much wanted the custody of the children, contrary to the father's false statement; this was agreed. The grandparents were rejected by their community because of their son's behaviour, but they managed to keep the children.

Another decision which would be virtually impossible to make without the help of an able, understanding and independent interpreter is to refer a child for special education. The class and language teachers and the Asian assistant make the initial suggestion to seek outside advice, after a considerable amount of thoughtful observation, and the parents then have to be consulted. This is a difficult matter, as it is for any parent and child, and without a mediator in the cases concerning Asian children, the situation would be intolerable.

Occasionally we are faced with the possibility of a battered or neglected child. S— was a boy with a speech defect. We suspected that he was an outcast in the family and there were signs of bruising and ill treatment. When the English social worker visited the house, the parents implied that they could not understand what was being said (we did not have an Asian assistant at the time) and so the circumstances remained unchanged.

After a year the boy was missing. He had been taken away by an uncle. On his return a thorough investigation was made and it was discovered that this child had been locked out at night and tied to a chair. He was not placed into care because of his language and culture; after their actions had been discovered the parents' attitudes towards him improved.

12 Staff and parents – school and home

I am often asked questions concerning the link between home and school. The answers to such questions can be neither brief nor straightforward.

Open evenings are held regularly, and on these occasions parents are able to discuss their children's work with the teachers. Although many of the parents of the immigrant and E2L children do attend, these evenings are only fringe links, and the relationships which are built up between the staff and parents involve a far greater understanding over a very long period.

Staff

First and foremost the atmosphere within the school must be a congenial one, and this is not always easy in an area where racial prejudice could exist, unseen though it may be. Staff must work together, share each other's problems and respect each other's points of view.

Some teachers will find it extremely difficult to work with E2L children who have language problems. They are qualified to teach reading and writing and may be very competent and interested in this field, when suddenly their experience and enthusiasm is rendered useless. In many cases teachers are able to adapt to the changed circumstances, but others cannot, and this fact should be recognised. Teachers in this situation should either be responsible for the indigenous children or transfer unashamedly to another area. To remain in a frustrated position and continually complain helps no one.

The staff should be able to express their opinions and difficulties concerning the immigrant and E2L children within reason, without feeling a sense of guilt. When parents mention a problem to me concerning a child of overseas parentage they sometimes conclude by adding, 'I'm not prejudiced' — the teaching staff should never feel the need to emphasise this fact with an almost defensive attitude.

I was involved in a discussion during a course on the multicultural society, and a young teacher was keen to accept advice concerning the children from minority groups in his class. He admitted at one point that he found the West Indians in his school difficult and immediately another teacher turned round and retorted, 'I can't think why, I don't.' I later discovered that she was married to a West Indian; she could have contributed some valuable information, but instead she left her colleague with a sense of inadequacy and guilt — he made no further comment.

As a young teacher there was a time when I too found the West Indian children difficult to control. I dreaded having them in my class, so much so that I went to the headmistress and pleaded for her not to give me a certain boy named Winston. She agreed, but did not let the matter rest. A few weeks later she suggested that I attend a week-end course organised by the Society of Friends on West Indian children. This I did, and it was one of the most valuable turning points in my teaching career. Throughout the week-end I met and spoke to many West Indian people who were engaged in work at all levels of education. In that short while I began to understand their culture and attitudes for the first time, and I enjoyed their company tremendously as I tried to view the school situation through their eyes. When the new term began Winston joined my class and I had no regrets.

A head teacher said to me once, 'I think it quite unnecessary to spend time studying the background and culture of these minority groups — they are living in England now — it is they who should study our culture and fit in with us.' Only through understanding each other's way of life can we hope to create and form a good relationship between races living alongside each other, and even if the children have been born in England, their parents are still very conscious of their native heritage and rightly so.

An adviser made the following comment to me: 'People willingly admit their inadequacies and failures when dealing with a subject, but it is quite a different matter to admit them when speaking of human relationships. Thus in some counties there are more advisers for the teaching of PE, Art or Mathematics than there are for teaching E2L children, even when schools have a high percentage of non-English speaking pupils.'

Attitudes towards other nationalities are very personal and it is impossible to generalise; it is also impossible to state categorically that there is no racial prejudice amongst the staff of a school. A person's feelings depend so much on his individual experiences, his politics and possibly his religious views.

A teacher from a neighbouring multicultural school came to see me. 'I feel so guilty,' she admitted. 'I enjoyed teaching the Indian children until suddenly my daughter started to go out with a Hindu boy, and now I just don't know what to do or think.'

On another occasion a member of staff told me that until recently she had had no ill feeling towards the 'immigrant' community, but her attitude changed when she discovered that an Indian family from outside the area was moving into a new house on the nearby estate, while her own daughter, who had been on the waiting list for years, still remained cooped up in a bed-sitting room. 'I just feel so hurt at the moment, but I shall get over it,' she remarked.

A dining helper asked to see me. 'Miss Brown, I've got no objection to the "immigrant" children in our school, but do you know, they have come into my garden and taken all my brussels sprouts. They say it is a compliment, they would have left them if they had not been good. What can I do?'

One of the school cleaners spoke to me. 'When I woke up this morning, I found an old bedstead on my compost heap. Whatever shall I do with it? My Indian neighbours are very nice, but I just can't have their rubbish.'

It is seldom the big things which cause feelings to rise and prejudice to creep in, it is the build up of the little everyday happenings, and staff must be able to share their difficulties.

Not only is such an understanding important for our own sakes, but it also gives us an appreciation of the difficulties and misunderstandings which arise in the local community. When members of staff are of different nationalities objective open discussion is particularly profitable. There should also be a realisation that similar problems do occur within the indigenous community, but, because the language and culture is understood, the difficulties can be more easily accepted or resolved.

The organisation and curriculum within the school should be planned according to the needs of the children and not only according to the academic expectations of the teachers. Pressures of work and discipline can quickly mount up when the balance of control and freedom is incorrect and additional strain is placed on the teacher.

Parents

The atmosphere in the school makes or mars the link with parents, for in a multiracial community the school is often the centre of the society and the one piece of neutral ground where everyone should be able to shed their grievances and work together.

Good sound relationships with parents take time. When the staff and parents speak different languages they have to develop a trust and understanding which reaches beyond words, and this may take several years.

One cannot generalise on ways to encourage parents into school, one can only look at the whole situation and discover the most successful methods through trial and error.

In the late nineteen-sixties, very few Indian mothers or grandmothers entered our school building, apart from on the first day when a child was admitted and his whole family would accompany him. We wondered how we could help the mothers to overcome their shyness, and finally decided to invite them to tea, asking them to bring a little of their own food to include with the tea and cakes which we provided. This proved to be successful, and every term thirty or forty Indian mothers ventured into the language room. However, after four or five years, a neighbouring factory opened a department especially for the Asian women, the mothers and older married sisters then left home at 8 a.m. and worked there all day. The tea parties were no longer a practical solution for meeting the mothers, although they continued to make the grandmothers welcome.

We then arranged evening meetings. Sometimes the mothers would be invited to look round the school with an interpreter, or the children would return with them and accompany them to the classrooms. We concentrated on the mothers because the fathers were either working or sleeping, and, even if they showed an interest in their child's books, they rarely spent time with their child.

Gradually the Asian families became accustomed to the school, but it was not easy.

One evening when a Ugandan Asian teacher was speaking to these parents in the hall, all the mothers suddenly laughed. I commented on this afterwards, and asked what they had found amusing. The teacher explained. She had said to the parents, 'You will find that the methods and equipment used here are very different from those

used when we were at school.' The mothers laughed. 'But we did not
go to school,' they chorused.

It is so easy for the well-meaning indigenous population to say that
immigrant women should attend the classes provided and learn to
speak English — maybe they forget that many of these people can
neither read nor write their own language.

For ten years I hoped that the mothers of the Asian children in our
school might feel the need, and summon up the courage to express a
desire, to learn to speak English. I realised that in our situation this
was a request which must come from them in their own time, for it
would not be an easy step to take. The deep reserve and shyness of
these mothers had to be overcome, they would need to submit themselves to a way of education which, in many cases, was hitherto unknown and often feared; and, perhaps the greatest hurdle of all, they
had to win the consent of their husbands, for without such an agree-
ment they would not be allowed to embark on even a simple course
connected with learning English.

Then in 1977, the first request was made. One of the mothers asked
my Asian assistant if there was a book containing Punjabi/English
phrases which she could buy in order to try to teach herself to speak
English.

We immediately seized the opportunity of offering help — not in
the form of a book, but in a friendly gathering in the language room
which included any mother who might be interested to join us for
simple lessons in the English language.

Within three days the word had spread. My assistant invited as many
mothers as she could, and on the following Wednesday ten of them
arrived. A friendly and relaxed hour was spent pretending to visit the
doctor. Provision had to be made for the babies and toddlers, but,
with the organisation of a rota of Asian mothers and the help of a
girl from the senior school, the children were happily occupied.

The number of mothers attending has been steadily maintained
and many topics have been covered in their 'lessons'. They have visited
the shops and the library, so that they too are experiencing English as
a living language. Two evening classes are now organised in the school
and several of the mothers who attend are linked with the Parosi
scheme.

'Parosi' is the Hindi word for 'neighbour' and a scheme with this
title has been promoted by the television to encourage English speaking adults to help Asian women living nearby to learn the English

language (it is a scheme similar to the adult literacy campaign launched a few years ago).

Unfortunately it is sometimes impossible to foresee a misunderstanding which can easily and quickly arise from a well-intentioned arrangement. After one of our Diwali celebrations a grandmother asked me if she could make a special festival recipe for our children similar to the one which she used to make for the children in her village back in the Punjab. I agreed for her to bring the food along to school on the Friday. It arrived during the morning in an enormous container, balanced on a push-chair. The old lady had taken a great deal of time and trouble to prepare the food which looked and tasted rather like rice pudding, and she assured me that she had included thirty pints of gold-top milk in the ingredients. The children thoroughly enjoyed tasting the recipe and the grandmother went home happy and satisfied. On the Monday, however, two Asian parents asked to see me, they were very worried and discussed their problem with me and my Asian assistant for over an hour. The parents explained to me that there could have been a spell in this pudding because the food had not been offered to God in a proper temple. Because we had celebrated Diwali in our hall the old lady had used the school as a temple (there was no recognised public place of worship for the Sikh community locally), but the parents were horrified at the idea. They told me that if a child died as a result of this action I would be held responsible — they implored me never again to allow an Asian person to supply food for their children — apart from cakes for the Christmas party.

Teachers should try not to be quick in criticising cultural differences. The West Indian extended-family system and common-law partnership can cause grave misunderstandings especially when children live with an aunt or grandmother in one house and the parents occupy another residence down the road. I have known several children who appear to accept this arrangement quite happily and explain that they live with their aunt because she hasn't any children of her own.

An attractive Asian teenager came to tell me about her forthcoming wedding. We had a long discussion concerning arranged marriages. 'I could never cope with the responsibility of choosing a husband and a house.' she explained. 'I'm glad my marriage is arranged for me. It is such a pity that you do not have this custom, then you would never have been left on the shelf!'

Criticism is sometimes levelled at the families of minority groups who request vegetarian meals at school or refuse to eat beef or pork. 'Why can't they fit in with us and our menus?' a visitor remarked. A Hindu, who worked in the Domestic Science department of a secondary school, said to me, 'I tried so hard to conform to your meat diet, but it was like asking you to eat a dog, and I could not do it.'

Cultural differences

Different forms of etiquette can cause misunderstanding and people are accused unjustly of rudeness.

A grandfather came to see me during a lunch hour and asked if his granddaughter could start school the following term. I explained that as she would not be five years of age, this was not possible. 'Then I will sit here until you agree,' he told me emphatically and seated himself opposite my desk refusing to move. This incident took place before I had an Asian member of staff, and I was not at all sure what to do. Finally I telephoned the Education Office, who eventually contacted an Asian teacher. He came over to the school and spoke to the gentleman concerned, explaining the situation.

He also explained to me that this grandparent was not being unduly rude; in the region of India from which he came, it was the practice to sit down and discuss a problem at length if a disagreement arose, and it always took place between men. I was at a great disadvantage being a woman in this particular situation, but the grandfather apologised for causing me any inconvenience, left with a warm hand-shake, and troubled me no further.

As understanding slowly develops, the members of the minority groups become less diffident and are willing to discuss their problems.

'We have no black or white children back home,' said a West Indian. 'We have just children — why is it not so here?'

A Sikh turned to me one afternoon after the local Sikh meeting place had been interfered with, and asked, 'We treat all men as brothers — why is it not so here?'

School and community — many cultures

Our Asian assistant has now forged and cemented a strong link between the school and the local Asian community. The Indian parents enjoy and participate in our communal activities. They contribute to and attend the Harvest festival, and afterwards some of the gifts are distributed to the elderly grandmothers, who understand that they are not accepting charity, but the fruits of thanksgiving.

The children of minority groups take a full part in our Christmas celebrations, and their parents (who as far as possible are welcomed in their own language) show a great deal of interest in the different events and support us in any way they can, particularly with sewing.

The climax of our celebrations as far as the Asian parents are concerned is the Diwali Festival of Light enjoyed by all, both young and old. The lighted candles, the saris and the music, the story told in Punjabi and the expressions of delight on the faces of three generations of the Asian community, create an atmosphere of warmth and unity which remains with us throughout the year.

Only recently the sound of Indian singing drifted up to my room. I soon located its source — the staff room! An Indian mother and grandmother were helping our Asian assistant in teaching some Indian dances to a group of girls for the forthcoming Diwali ceremony. No recorded music was needed, for the adults sang the accompaniment as they demonstrated the delicate feet and hand movements. We are hoping that more Asian mothers and grandmothers will come into school on a regular basis to help the children learn dances of their own culture and then introduce them to the English girls.

At the close of one Diwali service the Indian mothers handed me gifts of money. 'Please buy something for the teachers,' they said. After a little thought, I suggested using the money to buy new wallpaper for the staff room, which is also used by all the children when they come to watch the television programmes. The parents were delighted with the idea, and also with the result, which has brightened up a dark area, and reminds us continually of the overcoming of darkness with light, and evil with good.

It is so important for the mothers and older sisters to feel welcome in an infant school. They can more easily accept the strangeness of the building when surrounded by young children, and if they fail to enter the infant section, it is very unlikely that they will ever cross the thresholds of the junior and senior schools.

Many of these Asian mothers are carrying heavy and solitary burdens, and although it is outside the scope of teaching, we do try to listen to their problems and offer assistance and advice if we can, knowing that they rarely seek help elsewhere because of their uncertainty of communication and who to approach or where to go.

Immigrant families may live in overcrowded houses trying to share a kitchen or toilet with people of a different race and culture; others are isolated completely from their families, unable to communicate in any way with their relatives; some of the women are hit by their husbands or sons, others are rejected and despised.

An Italian mother explained to me how much harder it was to be cast aside by your family in a foreign country where there was no one of your own nationality in an official capacity to turn to for advice and support. As I write I recall a Chinese mother who suffered a mental breakdown and no one in the neighbourhood or hospital could speak her language.

Very often, if there is trouble in one particular family — and here I am not referring to death or illness — the family will be disowned by the rest of the community. An Indian father approached us and asked us where he could take his pregnant sixteen-year-old daughter for an abortion. The father of the baby was an English man, and the Asian family feared that if the news leaked out they would be rejected by their community because the girl's condition and the circumstances were such a disgrace to the culture. An abortion was not possible, but the girl was allowed to marry the baby's father and go to live with him.

Reports were brought to our notice concerning an Asian woman who was living in hiding at the back of a garage. The reports were true — she had been there for months following a broken marriage. The Social Services worked hard on her case and enabled her to return to India.

Two letters were received in school reporting another Asian mother who was shut indoors and being ill treated. She was unable to seek legal advice because of her inability to speak and read or write English, and her husband took advantage of the situation knowing that she was too frightened to call for help.

The work in the multicultural school can extend far beyond the boundaries of an academic syllabus, reaching out to the Asian who regularly visits the school during the lunch hour to have his mail translated, or the Indian widow who is seeking for an explanation of her late husband's will. But there is a limit to what we could or should do, and a point where we have to stop and remind ourselves that our task is to teach the children and not take on the role of a social worker. The Social Services, health visitors and police are very helpful, and a vital link should be maintained with them.

One afternoon an English mother ran into my classroom. 'Please can

I have Steven — his little sister has just hung herself on the garden fence — she is dead.'

On the following day the mother returned. 'Please let me stay in school for a while where it is quiet — my husband's relations are making such a noise wailing at home.'

Steven's father was a West Indian. His parents' marriage was a happy one, but at the point of tragedy each person had to express the outpouring of grief in his or her own way — it could not be otherwise.

Panya was a Greek girl. A welfare helper in the school asked me to watch her as she walked, and we noticed her unsteady sideways gait. I asked the mother to take her to the doctor.

Two weeks later Panya died in hospital after a major operation for a brain tumour. She was buried on her sixth birthday.

We knelt at the funeral service in the packed Greek Orthodox church, everyone was holding a candle and in the flickering light I looked at the many Greek mourners who surrounded me. Their piteous weeping and black garments left an indelible picture in my memory. On this occasion I was the foreigner, and yet how hard it was for me to recognise my position.

We kissed the white coffin, then filed through the door and on to the cemetery.

Panya was buried in her party dress, her birthday gifts were dropped down beside her. With her family I shared and tasted the 'heavenly food', and then the little coffin was covered.

Relations comforted the distraught father, but the mother stood silent and alone at the grave side.

I stepped forward and held out my hand, but immediately realised that my intuitive move was wrong. I had rudely intruded into a different culture, and my gesture was completely out of place.

Quietly I withdrew and left.

As teachers in multicultural schools our work is to educate the children in our care, but not transform them. We must have the courage of our convictions to open up avenues leading into the English language and culture, so that the children of other traditions may enter and move forward in our society, but we must never lose the integrity which enables us to recognise and respect those individual qualities which should remain untouched and unchanged — the rightful heritage of each nationality.

Bibliography

Bellugi, U. and Brown, R. (1964), *The Acquisition of Language*, Monograph of the Society for Research in Child Development, University of Chicago Press

Berlyne, D.E. (1970), 'Children's Reasoning and Thinking', in *Carmichael's Manual of Child Psychology* (Third edition), ed. P.H. Mussen, John Wiley

Bowker, G. (1968), *Education of Coloured Immigrants*, Longman

Bradford Infant Centres (1973), *English as a Second Language for the Five year old* (Third report), City of Bradford Educational Services Committee

Brittan, E.M. and Townsend, H.E.R. (1972), *Organisation in Multiracial Schools*, NFER.

Candlin, C and Derrick, J. (1970), *Education for a Multi-cultural Society, No. 2: Language*, CRC

Central Advisory Council for Education (1967), *Children and their Primary Schools* (The Plowden report), Vol. 1, HMSO

Cheetham, J. (1972), *Social Work with Immigrants*, Routledge and Kegan Paul

Chomsky, C. (1969), *The Acquisition of Syntax in Children from Five to Ten*, MIT Press

City of Bradford Metropolitan Council (1978), *Keystone: Bradford Infant Language Scheme* (Draft material)

Community Relations Commission (1974), *Educational Needs of Children from Minority Groups*, CRC

Community Relations Commission (1976), *Education and Community Relations*, Bulletin, March/April 1976, CRC

Department of Education and Science (1971), *The Education of Immigrants*, Education Survey 13, HMSO

Department of Education and Science (1972), *The Continuing Needs of Immigrants*, Education Survey 14, HMSO

Department of Education and Science (1976), *A Language for Life* (The Bullock report), HMSO

Derrick, J. (1966), *Teaching English to Immigrants*, Longman Group

Eyken, W. (1967), *The Pre-School Years*, Penguin

Garvie, E. (1976), *Breakthrough to Fluency*, Blackwell

Herriott, P. (1971), *Language and Teaching*, Methuen and Co., Ltd.

James, A.G. (1974), *Sikh Children in Britain*, Oxford University Press

Labov, W. (1964), *Social Dialects and Language Learning*, National Council of Teachers of English, Champaign, Ill.

Lawton, D. (1968), *Social Class, Language and Education*, Routledge and Kegan Paul

Lewis, M.M. (1963), *Language, Thought and Personality in Infancy and Child-hood*, Harrap and Co., Ltd.

Lewis, M.M. (1969), *Language and the Child*, NFER

Luria, A.R. and Yudavich, F.I. (1960), *Speech and the Development of Mental Processes in the Child*, Staples Press

MacNamara, J. (1966), *Bilingualism and Primary Education: A Study of Irish Experience*, Edinburgh University Press

McCarthy, D.A. (1954), 'Language Development in Children' in *A Manual of Child Psychology*, ed. L. Carmichael, John Wiley

McNeill, D. (1970), 'The Development of Language' in *Carmichael's Manual of Child Psychology* (Third edition), ed. P.H. Mussen, John Wiley

Menyuk, P. (1969), *Sentences Children Use*, Maple Press and Co.

Piaget, J. (1959), *The Language and Thought of a Child*, Routledge and Kegan Paul

Schools Council Working Paper 13 (1967), *English for the Children of Immigrants*, HMSO

Schools Council Working Paper 29 (1970), *Teaching English to West Indian Children*, Evans/Methuen Educational

Schools Council Working Paper 31 (1970), *Immigrant Children in Infant Schools*, Evans/Methuen Educational

Schools Council Working Paper 50 (1973), *Multiracial Education: Need and Innovation*, Evans/Methuen Educational

Scope Handbook 3, *English for Immigrant Children in the Infant School*, Longman

Slobin, D.I. (1971), *Psycholinguistics*, London Scott-Foreman

Templin, M.C. (1957), *Certain Language Skills in Children*, Minnesota ULP

Vygotsky, Lev. S. (1962), *Thought and Language*, MIT Press

Weir, R.H. (1962), *Language in the Crib*, Mouton, The Hague

Whorf, B.L. (1966), *Language, Thought and Reality*, ed. J.B. Carroll, Massachusetts Institute of Technology, Cambridge, Mass.

Wilkinson, A. (1971), *The Foundations of Language*, Oxford University Press

Woodward, P. (1973), *Education for a Multi-cultural Society*, No. 3, CRC

Index

171